Heaven's Formula

For Saving The World

Heaven's Formula For Saving The World
by Woo Myung

First Edition Published June 2013

Published by Cham Books
1202 Kifer Rd., Sunnyvale, CA 94086, USA
Tel: (408)475-8783
chambooks.inc@maum.org
www.chambooks.com

ISBN: 9781625930163

Library of Congress Control Number: 2013942835

This book has been translated into English from the original Korean text published in 2007. Translated by members of the Maum Meditation Translation Team.

All creative work, illustrations, and calligraphy (covered under copyright) are by the author.

Book Design by Color of Dream
Printed in Seoul, Korea

Heaven's Formula
For Saving The World

Woo Myung

Woo Myung, bestselling author of many books about Truth, attained enlightenment after deep introspection about life and existence. Once he became Truth, he dedicated his life to teaching others to become Truth and founded Maum Meditation. For his efforts, he was awarded the Mahatma Gandhi Peace Prize by the UN-NGO, International Association of Educators for World Peace (IAEWP) in September 2002. Woo Myung has also been appointed as a World Peace Ambassador by the same organization.

He is the author of numerous books including *World Beyond World, The Way To Become A Person In Heaven While Living, Nature's Flow, Mind, Where You Become True Is The Place of Truth, The Living Eternal World,* and *Stop Living In This Land. Go To The Everlasting World Of Happiness. Live There Forever* which have been published in English. *Stop Living In This Land. Go To The Everlasting World of Happiness. Live There Forever* reached No.1 on the Bestseller list of Amazon, the world's biggest online bookstore, in November 2012. His other books, *The Book Of Wisdom* and *The Enlightened World* are in the process of being translated into English as well as Japanese, Chinese, French, Italian, Spanish, Portuguese, German, and Swedish.

Contents

When the day is clear, people blame the world for it being too clear. They also blame the world when it is dark, for being too dark. They do not realize that the world and all creations in it exist by the providence of heaven and earth, that they themselves exist by the will of heaven and earth, and they ungratefully blame the world.

In the world, there is nothing and nobody to blame or fault.

Man does not know it is wrong in principle to believe he is right and other people are wrong. He does not know his destination, and even though he is lost wandering in a dream, he is unaware of it. In order to teach people that there is nothing that lasts or remains in matters of human life - a dream - I have come with the medicine that wakes people from their dreams.

In any case, even though it is silent, the clear blue sky, that is, heaven's providence, must have its reasons. The words and actions of people living in the world reflect what they hold in their minds; the way each person lives is an expression of his mind.

Six years ago I founded Maum Meditation which led many people to enlightenment. In order to bring the method to the wider world, I came to America - the capital of the world - and introduced Maum Meditation to people from all walks of life. When I met with the Chairman of the U.N. General Assembly I stressed that the only way for mankind to have true peace is to make the minds of all people become one.

I traveled around America and many other countries, opening Maum Meditation centers and introducing Maum Meditation to people. And I am still traveling, waiting for the day when the reality of people living in falseness with suffering and burden changes to that of everybody becoming one and Truth; the day when we all live in the true world.

There are people with positive mind-sets, good people, all over the world, and some of them are already seventy, eighty years old. Finding Truth and becoming Truth before they pass away is a matter of life and death for them. Consequently, there is never a time when I do not feel the urgency of having to reach as many places as I can in this wide world.

I introduce people to the way, the method, for man to become complete and for mankind to become one, and teach them how it can be done. I wrote this book and I continue to travel, in the hope that all people will meditate and become complete.

Part 1

From Enlightenment
To Spreading Truth
In The World

On my way to *Moon-gyung*, which was the first time I set out to spread Truth, there was a rainbow in front of me the entire way - as if to raise my down-trodden spirits. And while we were meditating in *Moon-gyung*, there was a rare and strange cloud in the sky.

From Enlightenment
To Spreading Truth In The World

I was conceived during the Korean civil war, and I was born around the time South Korean troops retaliated to the first North Korean invasion.

There were two mountains near my hometown where I spent my childhood, Mount *Bongwoojae* and Mount *Ansan*. My village was almost right in the middle of the two, and during the war my village became a battleground with North Korean troops camped in *Bongwoojae* and South Korean troops in *Ansan*. When the war ended, we often found remnants from the battles around the village.

A few of the older children died while playing with grenades that had been left behind. There was also a time when my friends and I went to the stream to catch fish and found human bones. We had dammed up a spot filled with fish but when we found the bones, we broke the dam and let all the fish go. We also often found human bones while gathering firewood in the mountains, as well as bullets and used cartridges. It was a time of abject poverty; due to the civil war that broke out just five years after Korea became free from Japanese rule, everyone at the time, from all those older than me to those ten years younger, worried about where their next meal was coming from and how to survive.

My older brothers all died of smallpox at a young age, and with just three daughters until I was born, I was a much-cherished son. My father also passed away when I was nine, and we were one of the many sorrow-filled families of that time.

In the olden days, the family paid respects to the deceased for three years, at a place called *binsoe*. We lay food at my father's table every morning and night and it was during this time that I began thinking about the futility of life, where people come from, why we live, and where we go after we die.

I had read many scriptures by the time I reached my mid-thirties, but I had not found any answers that satisfied me. I decided to find the answers to these questions on my own. I spent those years with the constant thought in the back of my mind that after I earned a lot of money, I would go and live in a cottage near a mountain stream and meditate on Truth until I became enlightened.

I sought out many sages and ascetics while living in the world, but no one truly knew Truth - there were just many who pretended to know. In Mount *Jiri*, there was a person who told me to focus my consciousness in the middle of my forehead. I also tried various Buddhist meditations and there were places that asked me to throw away my thoughts.

In my life, everyone was my teacher; my parents, my teachers, my friends, everybody around me as well as everything that I saw.

One day, I had a vision while I was meditating at home. In the vision I was coming down from the mountains to *Gechon* Lake (literally meaning the lake where the heavens open), which was between my hometown and the town where my mother's family lived. At the time, I was forty-one years old. I could not easily forget this vision and it was always vividly in my mind.

I ran a college preparatory tuition academy and I earned enough to be financially comfortable. Towards the end of 1995 and around the beginning of 1996, I made up my mind to take a vacation during some public holidays and go to *Mount Gaya* and seek Truth. On the 3rd of January, 1996, I was enlightened that I am Truth and that my destiny is to save the world by teaching Truth.

I met with Jesus Christ, *Shakyamunyi* and many other saints in heaven. From then on, I had the ability to see with the eyes of heaven, and hear with the ears of heaven; although I knew absolutely nothing, at the same time there was nothing I did not know and all my previous questions disappeared.

I continued to study Truth diligently while running my preparatory tuition academy. When I, a true fool, came to know everything, the feeling of frustration in my chest cleared, and absorbed in the fun of knowing Truth, I stayed up many nights, writing and writing. At the time, I published a book called "The Book of Wisdom" and many people who read the book sought me out at the academy. I bought them dinner, gave them a place to sleep, and talked to them about Truth.

During that time, I told more than a hundred people about the way to become enlightened. I told them to go home, diligently practice the method and return when they had become enlightened. Months passed by, and no one came back. So in November of 1996, I rented out a room at an inn located in *Sun-yoo-dong, Moon-gyung*, and taught the method to around ten people.

I was very reluctant, and afraid, to teach and spread Truth. I wanted people to meditate and become enlightened on their own if possible and since I was earning a fair amount of money through the academy, I thought I could simply continue to earn more and provide them with a place to meditate. On my way to *Moon-gyung*, which was the first time I set out to spread Truth, there was a rainbow in front of me the entire way - as if to raise my down-trodden spirits. And while we were meditating in *Moon-gyung*, there was a rare and strange cloud in the sky which the meditation students looked at in wonder.

A week later, nine of the ten people who had come were enlightened of the first level. They were so overcome with joy, they did not know what to do with themselves and we drank and partied.

A month later, I taught the method in *Un-yang, Kyung-nam*. Word had spread that people were attaining enlightenment and more than fifty people came. A month after that, I taught the method in *Moongyung-Saejae*, and later on, I rented a student dormitory in Mount *Gaya*.

What began as one session every month quickly became two sessions and then two sessions became four. In the beginning, in order to attract many people to come, I gave a lot of people the abilities to see and hear with the eyes and ears of heaven. They were able to see heaven, and hear the messages of heaven.

Fortune-tellers from all over the country came when people heard this news.

When fortune-tellers become possessed by the spirits that enable them to foresee certain things, they suffer physical pain. I asked them if they wanted to be rid of the spirits and many said yes. Not long after I drove the spirits out of them, one of the fortune-tellers came back and asked me to reattach the spirit that had been in him. He told me that without the spirit, he could not earn a living for his family because he could not forsee the future. So I reattached it for him.

Many people who came in those early days sought Truth so that they could brag about what they know or to become a superior version of themselves. These motivations stemmed from their strongly fixed frames of minds and many of them gave up meditation when things did not work out the way they wanted. The ability to see heaven and hear heaven had come to them before they had become completely enlightened to the Truth and because they still had their own minds, they were not able to meditate further due to their remaining selves.

Every week in those first few years, I opened the path to these abilities for 10-20% of the people who came. Many people gathered on the weekends to meditate because they wanted to receive these abilities and they found it fascinating to hear the news of heaven.

In this way, I guided many people through the first level of the meditation, but soon I realized that they still had their own false minds. I became enlightened of the method for the second level - the method to realize that human minds do not exist - and began to teach people.

After people completed the second level, they were enlightened that human minds do not exist, but they thought that nothing exists after death. I realized I needed to find a method to teach them of existence. At this time, heaven showed me the scene of my death and the scene of life. I realized that this meant one has to die and I began to teach people how to discard their very selves.

I taught the first level in Mount *Gaya*, and the second level in *Hajam*, *Kyung-nam*. When we were in *Hajam*, I made a miracle happen: pillars of fire shot up in the sky near the place where we were meditating and the next day it was reported in the local papers. Everyone who was meditating at the time cried out with wonder when they saw the pillars of fire.

I taught the first level in Mount *Gaya*, and the second level in *Hajam*, *Kyung-nam*. When we were in *Hajam*, I made a miracle happen: pillars of fire shot up in the sky near the place where we were meditating and the next day it was reported in the local papers.

Everyone who meditated was cured of any illnesses he had. When people became free from the suffering of their minds, they were also cured of their physical illnesses. For a period of time afterwards, I often cured people of their illnesses in front of hundreds of people watching.

After people practiced the third level, they were enlightened that the Universe is within them. However, they still did not know the Universe's body and mind, or in other words, *Jung* and *Shin*, which is the origin of the Universe. Thus I taught them the next level and brought them to enlightenment. Then came the fifth level, when one comes to know that in the Universe there is the one God, who is the only existence in the world and that one's self is this very existence. I also brought people to enlightenment in the sixth level that when God of the entire Universe and the land of God are within one's self, heaven is right where he is. In the seventh level, one surrenders all of his self to the Universe so that only the Creator and God which is Truth remains, and this existence becomes his mind. When he is then reborn as the body and mind of Truth, he is the eternal and invincible Energy and Light of the Universe, which is life itself.

God has already given us all salvation, and heaven is within one's self. That is to say, within one's self there is God and the land of God. Thus, for such a person it is a new world - a new heaven and new earth - because he is reborn as God and has gone to everlasting heaven while his body is still living.

It is a new heaven and a new earth when man is reborn as God into the land of God. This is the eighth level. In the seventh and eighth level, God is within one's self so it is possible to converse freely with God. Since one's consciousness has changed to the consciousness of God that is life, he knows everything because he is wisdom itself. God's words are wisdom, and he is able to hear and know the words of God through wisdom.

To have the seal of God on one's forehead is none other than his mind becoming God. In Korean this is called *hon-jool* and it is a sign that God has entered his mind.

What someone has in his mind can be seen in his thoughts. There are over six billion people in the world but no two minds are alike. Thoughts are the expressions of what one has or holds in his mind. His mind exists in his clump, or mass, of thoughts.

For a person who has become one with God of the Universe, the pathway from the Universe to God within is wide open. In other words, he is connected as one with God of the Universe through his forehead. Such a person is one who has been given *hon-jool* for God comes forth from the forehead of a person who has God within.

The next stage is for the whole body to become light itself. A person who has become one with the great Soul and Spirit of the Universe is reborn as light itself.

Then, if one is enlightened that his body itself is complete, he is the great Universe's Soul and Spirit that is Truth, so the thought that his body existed in the past completely disappears. This is the sign that he has been completely born as Truth itself.

The Universe is originally one: the great Soul and Spirit. A person who has become this existence itself does not die - he has achieved human completion and lives forever. This is the seventh and eighth level and it took eight years to take people to this stage.

In the first, second, third, fourth, fifth and sixth level, one has only one enlightenment at each level but in levels seven and eight, one can be enlightened from everything he sees and hears and every time he thinks.

If one is completely enlightened, in other words, if he has died completely, he becomes Truth itself; and when he drinks the water of life from Truth, his self is forgotten completely.

Perfect Truth is the place where all knowing has ceased. It is the place where there is absolutely nothing that one knows, and there are no questions, doubts or suspicions. Such a person lives without false minds, and he does not store anything he does in his mind. His is the mind of God, so he just lives.

The way to Truth can only be reached if one discards all of his questions, his need to know, and knowledge itself. He must cast off these delusions and only when he discards even the curiosity of knowing, can Truth be the only existence remaining. When there is absolutely nothing in his mind, when his mind is the state where everything has ceased, there is no knowledge in his mind but at the same time a person who has become Truth will know all Truth.

There is enlightenment only in levels seven and eight. This is because only then does one become the consciousness of God and is reborn as God; therefore he is wisdom itself.

In the previous levels, one comes to know as much as his mind has been cleansed, as much as his mind has expanded, but true enlightenment of knowing everything only comes to a person in the seventh and eighth levels. A person in these levels does not have any obstacles or blockages, and is omniscient and omnipotent. He knows all of Truth that is righteousness. Only a person who has done levels seven and eight has been reborn with God's consciousness; and only he who has drunk from Truth's water of life is an enlightened person. He is a person who has achieved everything and he is complete.

Part 2

How To Become Truth And Why One Must Not Fail To Reach Truth

If one does not become Truth, he is dead inside a non-existent illusion that is just like a dream. But if he does become Truth, his self that has become Truth lives forever in the land of Truth. Is there anything more important than living?

How To Become Truth And Why One Must Not Fail To Reach Truth

How can one become Truth?
And why must one succeed in reaching Truth?

First, we must understand what Truth is. What is Truth? We have learned that Truth is everlasting and never-changing. So then, what is this eternal and never-changing existence? Let's begin by thinking about the Universe. The Universe is infinite so it cannot be drawn but let's represent it in this way.

The sky - the Universe - contains the stars, sun, moon and Earth; and on the Earth there are people. What you see and hear, everything just as it exists, is Truth; thus, what you see here is everything that exists in the Universe.

 In the Universe, there are stars, the sun, the moon and the Earth. Let us try thinking about things in the following way:

Imagine we, along with the stars, sun, moon, and Earth, went back in time to an eternity ago. Scientists tell us that the life-span of a star ranges from 5 to 14 billion years. The life-spans of stars, sun, moon, Earth, and man are like a split second compared with eternity. Therefore we would have all disappeared with the passing of time, so that now, at the present time, nothing would remain but the pure emptiness.

Now imagine that a fire burned this emptiness at 100 billion degrees Celsius for an eternity, to the present. This existence - the emptiness - would still just exist.

 This emptiness, which is the Universe before the infinite Universe, is Truth. Without a beginning or an end, it is a living existence that existed an eternity ago and will continue to exist for an eternity after.

Just as we have bodies and minds, this infinite Universe or sky also has a body and mind. Its body is the complete emptiness, and its mind is the sole God who is omnipresent throughout the entire Universe.

The reason we cannot see God of the Universe is man has self-centered attachments, a mind that is the same shape and form as his body. Because of his mind, he cannot see, know or become the great Soul and Spirit, which is the body and mind of the Universe. One must become this great Soul and Spirit in order to see, know and become it. Man cannot become one with Truth because of his self-centered attachments, which are his sins.

 This great Soul and Spirit is the Creator. It is this huge Soul and Spirit that created the stars in the sky, the sun, the moon, the Earth, all creations and mankind.

In science class, we learned that the stars, the sun,

the moon, and the Earth came from the Universe, as we also did. This is the Soul and Spirit of Truth. Unless man returns to this existence of Truth - the Soul and Spirit - he cannot live forever.

The way to become this existence itself, the great Soul and Spirit, is to discard the self-centered human mind as well as the body that contains it.

 And when one's delusional Universe is also discarded, only this existence remains. When one's mind becomes this existence and he is reborn, he is reborn as the child of God. This is resurrection and eternal life. This Soul and Spirit is him; and he is Truth itself.

When one is reborn as this existence, he lives as the immortal Truth, because the whole is him, the individual; and the individual is the whole.

Heaven only exists for a person who has become Truth, the great Soul and Spirit of the Universe. Man's mind is only as big as his body; when it becomes as big as the great Soul and Spirit of the Universe, he lives forever in heaven. But in order for this to happen, he must discard his body, mind and even the Universe through

the Maum Meditation method and become Truth, the great Soul and Spirit of the Universe which is eternal and immortal. Only then has he achieved human completion. It is from this place that the Bible, the Buddhist scriptures and all other scriptures were written.

Now that we understand what Truth is, I will explain heaven and hell.

The difference between heaven and hell is as follows: heaven is the place where the great Soul and Spirit of the Universe, Truth, lives; whereas hell is the place where one only knows what he has experienced in his life, and where he lives enslaved to the mind of those shadows.

Last night, I dreamt I was in a battlefield. Gunfire was coming from all directions and all of my fellow soldiers were killed. I decided to flee and hide, but in order to do so I had to run to the mountains fifty miles up ahead. Having been shot in the left leg, I began limping towards my destination. Not realizing I was dreaming, the pain I felt seemed so real - all night long, I dreamt of running around, limping in the battlefield under a shower of never-ending gunfire. As I finally reached the mountains, I was shot by the enemy. At that moment, I woke up from my sleep and realized that

I was not in the battlefield; there had been no gunfire, and I had not been shot. The dream was an illusion.

Although dreams exist, they are not real - they are illusions that do not actually exist. Man's life is like the dream he dreams at night during which he believes it to be real. Man lives in the shadow of his memories - self-centered attachments he has in his mind - which are the experiences he has gained from the life he has lived. In other words, man's life is a dream, and thus he lives in a dream-like state of mind.

Suppose one has been living his life, and that at this moment, he is forty years old. Even if he continues to live to the age of ninety, he will continue to live with the same mind he has had until now. Furthermore, he will live on with that same mind even after death.

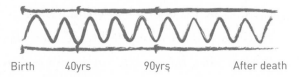

Birth   40yrs   90yrs   After death

That mind is a dream. That mind is hell. It is a dream that exists and yet does not because like all illusions, it is not real. And it is here, in such an illusion, that man lives due to his mind. Man cannot live as Truth unless he is reborn as the infinite Soul and Spirit that created the Universe, the everlasting Truth. Maum

Meditation's eight levels allow one to achieve this.

The false world

The origin

The true world

Level 1	Level 2	Level 3	Level 4	Level 5	Level 6	Level 7	Level 8
The level of knowing one is the Universe	The level of knowing there are no human minds	The level of knowing the Universe exists within oneself	The level of knowing the body and mind of the Universe	The level of seeing and knowing the infinite Universe consists of the original body and mind	The level of seeing and knowing heaven	Becoming the original body and mind	Being born in complete heaven; having the conscious-ness of heaven thereby being sealed on the forehead and becoming the body of light and knowing that one is complete
Mind (Karma)		Body (Habit)		The level of seeing and knowing		The level of achieving	

 In order to be reborn as both Energy and Light, which are the eternal and never-changing Soul and Spirit of the infinite Universe:

One must first eliminate his body, mind, and even the Universe.

Then, only the great Soul and Spirit remains. It is when the great Soul and Spirit becomes him that he is born again.

And so he is Truth; he, himself, is the stars, the sun, the moon, the Earth, all creations and mankind. Therefore, everything and everyone becomes Truth and lives forever. This place, this state of being, is heaven.

These are the eight levels of Maum Meditation. Simply put:

When you subtract your body and mind from the Universe, and the delusional Universe also disappears, pure emptiness remains. When you are born again as the emptiness, which is the great Soul and Spirit of the Universe, it is heaven and eternal life. Even if, at this very moment, an earthquake split the ground under your feet and you fell into the lava below, the Universe would still just exist. Therefore, so long as you have completely become the Universe, you who have become the Universe will live forever.

This is the way to human completion, and the way to transcend all religions. It is man becoming God and thus becoming complete. Such a world is the world beyond; it is the perfect, religion-transcending solution for the future. Then the whole of mankind would become one; everyone would regard others as oneself and would live for others. They would live eternally without death because they would be the great Soul and Spirit itself - the Energy and Light of the Universe. The reason man is born into the world is to be reborn as this existence.

God originally created a complete world but man is dead because of his own delusions. Maum Meditation allows one to become free from this and return to the Creator that is complete. The Soul and Spirit of the Universe is alive so if one becomes the wisdom of the great Soul and Spirit itself, he will be able to see and know the world as it truly is. All people would become saints and live forever in the true world of Truth.

All religions will become complete when man abandons his self. Furthermore, it is when he abandons his self and becomes Truth that he becomes complete. One must discard his sinful self instead of blaming other people, and he must become Truth so that he can live in heaven. Now is the moment we must seize, for it is the period of the Universe when those who have become complete may live in heaven.

If one does not become Truth, he is dead inside a non-existent illusion that is just like a dream. But if he does become Truth, his self that has become Truth lives forever in the land of Truth. So therefore, deciding whether or not to do this practice of the mind places a person at the crossroads of life and death. Is there anything more important than living? There is nothing more urgent than this.

It is absurd to believe that a person who is not reborn in heaven while he is alive can go to heaven after he is dead. Simply put, he cannot. When one's consciousness becomes one with the great Soul and Spirit of the Universe while he is alive, the world in which he lives is both heaven as well as eternal life, itself. That is why it makes no sense to say that a person who is not reborn in heaven while living could possibly enter heaven after death.

They say it is through faith that one may enter heaven. However, it is only when heaven exists in one's mind that he truly has faith.

이광식으로는 간식있어 돌릴때까지
곰처럼 있어 바란다

Stay put like a bear until you have solved the formula because it can
get you to Truth.

Part 3

The Dawning Of A New World
Is The Dawning Of
A New Consciousness

The dawning of a new world is the dawning of a new consciousness. It is a new world because there is no self and one becomes the Creator's consciousness itself. When he is reborn as this consciousness, it is a new world because heaven and earth exists within man.

The Sky Is The Stage
And The Creations Are The Actors

Many things may come and go in the empty space of the sky,

but the sky always just exists.

This sky is the mother and father of all creations;

it raises and rears all creations,

and it is also the stage.

Numerous actors may come and go on this stage,

but the stage is always just there.

Heaven and earth are drawings,

as are the sky and sea.

All creations on earth are drawings -

everything is a drawing.

When those drawings do not exist,

only the origin - the paper - remains.

When I am reborn as the paper, I am the master of all creation.

I am the origin, for I am reborn within myself,

and I am the master, because I am reborn within myself.

Whether I come or go,

I, who have become real, always just exist.

Ignorant Man

Mankind is lost because people lack wisdom. Not only are people ignorant of the true meaning of the religious scriptures, they do not know when they are being lied to. They are not able to differentiate between truth and lies. They believe in words that are not true when they are spoken in a grand manner. In other words, people live being fooled.

Man lives inside his mind, so he only agrees with things that suit his mind. When something does not suit it, he disagrees. He is unable to distinguish between what is true and false because his mind is self-centered. Truth knows falseness, but man's mind does not - this is the reason it is said man does not have wisdom. He does not even try to strive towards wisdom.

The Stage Is The Sky And The Sky Is The Stage

Regardless of what comes and goes on the stage,

the stage is always just there.

The people of the world are all actors,

but if they own the stage, they become the masters.

As masters, they will always be able to act on the stage.

The Delusional Universe And The True Universe

The Universe in a delusional mind is not the Universe of Truth. The Universe of a delusional mind does not exist inside that mind; the person and the Universe exist separately.

Hell is when man's delusion lives in a delusional Universe.

When a person becomes one with the land of Truth, when he has become heaven itself, the place to which he has "gone" is heaven. Heaven is where such a person lives.

The End Of The World

It has been said that the world will come to an end, and that at that time salvation will come.

People have no idea what the end of the world and salvation truly mean. There are countless books in bookstores but none of them are able to explain the true meaning of these words; when they do explain them it is done in a conceptual or abstract way that leads people further away from the true meaning.

There have always been earthquakes. People believe the world will come to an end through natural disasters or wars but these things will not cause the end of the world. The end of the world is a new age when those whose minds, whose consciousnesses, have become one with God - the infinite Universe and Creator - will live, while those who have not, will die.

Whether people live or die depends on whether or not their minds have changed to the mind of God. Those whose minds have changed to the mind of God will live forever in the new world, but those who are trapped inside their delusions are dead because their delusions are false; like a dream, they do not exist though they may seem to exist. Such a state is death itself and hell.

A person with a pure mind will know that the true way is to cleanse his mind and become Truth. However, a person with a dark mind will not know that at this time of the world's end, cleansing his mind will decide whether he lives or dies. He will not know because such a person is self-oriented and greedy, concerned only with his current life such as acquiring more possessions or bettering his circumstances.

If one lives with a mind full of attachments, he dies within those attachments. A person who is free from the mind of attachments and becomes the Energy and Light of the great Universe - Truth itself - does not die because he is Energy and Light.

It is the end of the world for those who do not become Truth. Those who are Truth will live eternally in the new world. Even after their bodies disappear, their Souls and Spirits will live in the land of Truth. For a dead person, it is the end of the world.

The end of the world exists for all those whose consciousnesses have not been born as Truth. When there is a dawning of a new consciousness; when one's consciousness has "opened"; when one's consciousness becomes complete; that is, when one has transformed as Truth, he will live.

For those who do not have Truth within them, it is death and the end of the world. The end of the world does not exist for those who have eliminated all creations in heaven and earth and have been reborn in the new heaven and new earth - in the land of the Creator that is Truth.

People think the end of the world is everything dying, but the end of the world is being reborn as Truth and living in heaven. It is the end of the world because one destroys heaven, earth and man with his mind, and because heaven, earth and man no longer exist, it is a new world.

When One Drinks The Water Of Life,
His Past Self Will Be Forgotten

It is often said that when one dies and drinks water from the spring of life, he will completely forget the past.

When man becomes free from his conceptions and habits, in other words, when he has no self and he becomes Truth itself by completely dying, his past self disappears and he is Truth so he has "drunk from the spring of life".

If one's mind does not exist and he has within him the great Soul and Spirit of the Creator, that is, if he has the Spirit of the Creator within him, he has been "sealed on the forehead" by the Spirit - he becomes one with the Spirit of the Universe. Such a person will know that material things which exist in the world and the real existence - the Creator's Soul and Spirit which is non-material - are one. He himself is the Creator's great Soul and Spirit itself and thus his whole body is connected with the great Soul and Spirit. He knows that existence (what is material) and non-existence (what is not material) are simply one, and he has become this oneness.

The next stage is to be enlightened that he himself is complete Truth. This enlightenment comes when he has no human minds whatsoever and he has become one with Truth itself.

Such a person is the completely living Soul and Spirit, the Energy and Light, of the great Universe. He who has become such is the water of life; therefore he does not have a past, and he does not even have the thought that he existed in the past. No matter how much he looks at his body and tries to think that it existed from the past, such thoughts do not exist in him. Furthermore, that past simply does not exist. Drinking the water of life means one completely forgets the past – it is to die completely, and when one's past self does not exist, it is to become Truth; to become life; and to become the Universe's Energy and Light.

When one drinks the water of life, one completely forgets his past self.

The Dawning Of A New World
Is The Dawning Of A New Consciousness

The apocalypse has always been a much discussed topic, and it is said that when it happens everyone will die. It is also often said that there will be a new world. New religions have often misinterpreted what "a new world" and "apocalypse" mean; and many people have taken these phrases quite literally, with some going as far as living their lives according to these wrong literal misinterpretations.

These days, mass communication has developed to the point where we are able to watch what is happening around the world on television the same day it happens. For example, we can hear about the death of an elephant in Africa on the day it died, and wherever we look, there are stories of people dying. There have always been earthquakes and they still happen in the present. Although it is believed that the meaning of "a dawning of a new world" is that the world will turn inside out, the true meaning is that the world - heaven and earth - will reopen. To reopen does not mean that heaven and earth will change. What it means is that whereas previously heaven, earth and man existed separately, the heaven and earth will exist in man, and that man will become the master of heaven and earth.

The huge Universe consists of a Soul and Spirit, or *Jung* (body) and

Shin (mind) respectively. The Universe is also called *Haneol* (which means the Universe, God).

When one is reborn as this *Jung* and *Shin*, he is the eternal and never-changing Energy and Light of the Universe. Therefore he lives forever, he does not ever die, the concept of you and me disappears, the concept of your country and my country disappears, no one has worries or woes, and this place, here, is paradise and heaven. For such a person, this place, here, is completeness that is the land of the origin - the land of the Soul and Spirit. He is the very Soul and Spirit of the Universe, and he lives forever, born as its *Jung* and *Shin*.

The dawning of a new world is the following:

When one completely discards his mind and body that comes from his self-centered mind that is the size of his form, and he is reborn as the infinite *Jung* and *Shin* that is Truth, all religions, ideologies and philosophies will unite.

It is the dawning of a new consciousness because our minds and bodies, or in other words, our Souls and Spirits, are reborn; and it is the dawning of a new world because instead of man existing separately from heaven and earth, they will become one and exist within man.

The dawning of a new world is the dawning of a new consciousness. It is a new world because there is no self and one becomes the Creator's consciousness itself. When he is reborn as this consciousness, it is a new world because heaven and earth exists within man.

Put in another way, when the illusionary heaven and earth that exists within one's mind is completely destroyed and eliminated, Truth that is the new heaven and earth becomes him, and he lives reborn in this land. Therefore it can be said that heaven and earth "reopens" and that it is a "new" world.

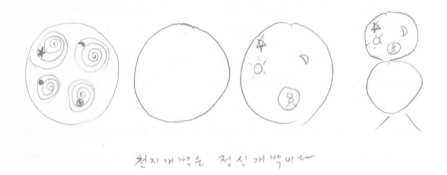

천지 개벽은 정신 개벽이다

The dawning of a new world is the dawning of a new consciousness.

Man Lives According To What He Has In His Mind

There are roughly seven billion people on this planet, but no two minds are alike.

The mind that one has is the following:

A person lives out his life according to his form and shape, and as he does so he "eats" or stores everything he sees, hears and feels, from his childhood with his parents to his surrounding environment, friends, kindergarten, elementary, middle and high school, college life and life in society.

The size of that cumulative mind is as big as his body - his shape and form. It is from within the boundaries of this mind that he judges right and wrong, good and evil, and discerns everything around him. All of these things are formed through the experiences of his life.

If he has lived with a certain kind of mind until the present, he will live with that delusional mind until the day he dies, and even after death.

Suppose a person studies law, information technology, or mechanical engineering. It is through the things he stores inside his mind that he will later eventually earn a living. His personality also shows what kind of things he has put inside his mind. The lives people live reflect what they have put inside their minds.

The education that we receive in schools is a worldly one, while cleansing one's mind is the education to become Truth. If Truth exists within man, he will live a life of Truth because he is Truth. In the same way, if heaven exists within a person, he will live in heaven because he has heaven in him. Because people live to the extent of what they have in their minds, a person who amasses blessings in heaven will live forever in heaven with those blessings.

Jesus Christ told us that a foolish person amasses fortune on earth while a wise person amasses treasures in heaven. This means it is worthless to amass one's fortune here on earth for his own sake - for the sake of his body or for his children - because this world is a dead world. For a person who amasses fortune in heaven, his fortune is his forever and he lives with as much as he has amassed. Each person who has been born as Truth has his own heaven, so each must make and amass his own blessings in that land.

Blessings should not be sought, but made and built. One lives in the eternal world with as much blessings as he has made and amassed. One lives eternally with as much blessings as he has in the land of Truth that is his mind.

Man Cannot See Truth

Every time a seminar or lecture is held in the U.S. I ask people if they know what the existence of Truth is, but no one knows.

Those who study the philosophy of *dō* call the existence of Truth "*dō*". Christians call Truth "God" and in Buddhism, it is called "Buddha". In Korea, it is called "*Haneol-nim*", and elsewhere it is also called "Allah".

This existence is alive, and it is eternal, never-changing and without death. Everything in the world was created by this existence of Truth; it is the Creator of the Universe. The land of this existence is the complete land of the Creator.

The reason man cannot see Truth is it can only be seen if man becomes the Creator and Truth. This eternal and never-changing existence of Truth is the infinite empty space of the Universe.

Let us draw the infinite Universe like this and think about things from this perspective.

 In the Universe, there are stars, the sun, the moon, the Earth, all creations and people.

Now let us suppose that all these things have been eliminated.

Even so, this existence, the empty space, which existed an eternity ago, still exists in the present and it will exist an eternity afterwards.

This existence is Truth. This existence is eternal and indestructible and it is the great living Soul and Spirit of the Universe.

This existence is the Creator and it is this existence that created all creations. It created the stars in the sky, the sun, the moon, the Earth, everything on Earth and people.

It is in order to find this existence that Christians take part in early morning and all night prayers, as well as practicing meditation in the mountains, but they have been unsuccessful. Buddhists also take part in all night meditation, as well as trying many other forms of meditation, but they too have been unable to find this existence. If they had, many people would have already become Truth.

All that man has is a mind of attachments, which is the same size as his body - his shape and form.

He is unable to see the Creator because he does not have Truth of this great Universe, the Creator, within him. The Creator, or Truth, can only be seen when one's mind becomes as big as the Creator that is Truth.

When man gets rid of his body and his mind of attachments - his self - and discards the Universe of his conceptions, Truth remains; and this Truth becomes his mind. Then, he is able to see Truth.

He is able to see Truth when he is enlightened that the entity of his self has disappeared from the Universe, and the delusional Universe of his conceptions has been discarded.

If one sees Truth, the Universe, while one still has a self, then that Universe is one of non-existence, but if he sees the Universe when none of his self exists, having become the Universe itself, the Universe has a great Soul and Spirit - *Jung* and *Shin*. This *Jung* and *Shin* is the body and mind of the Universe, respectively. All creations of the world are the representations of this existence of Truth, the Creator.

If asked what Truth looks like, the answer would be that all creations are Truth.

The original existence of Truth is the emptiness, but all things that have been created as the children of this existence are also Truth themselves. The material and the non-material are simply one. Everything is Truth. Man cannot see Truth because he has a narrow, self-centered mind of attachments that is the size of his shape and form. He will be able to see Truth when his mind is as big as the

Creator that is Truth. Only when his self no longer exists and he becomes this existence itself can he see this existence and become it.

Only A Sage Can Recognize A Sage; A Divine Being Cannot Be Seen By Man; Only A Person Who Has Become Truth Can Know Truth; A Living Person Can Distinguish The Living From The Dead But A Dead Person Cannot

The expressions in the title above mean one must become the very existence of what he desires to know in order to truly know it.

No one in the world knows the possessions of the people who pass him on the street, what belongings they have or their states of mind. Similarly, one must first become a sage in order to recognize a sage.

Man cannot see divine beings because divine beings are also human-beings. In order for man to recognize that a person is a divine being, he must be a divine being himself. One can only know Truth when he has become Truth, and a living person is a person who has become Truth. A person who has become Truth, that is, a person who is alive, will recognize who has become Truth and is therefore, alive. It is because his consciousness is alive that he is also able to know and recognize who is dead.

A person who is dead does not know what life and death is; his consciousness is dead so he is unable to tell who is living and who is dead. What this means is that a person of Truth knows both who has become Truth and who has not, while a person who has not become Truth does not know who is Truth. Because he is not Truth, he does not know that he is dead, nor can he recognize anyone else who is dead.

People cannot recognize divine beings for who they are.
Only a *dō-in* can recognize a *dō-in*. If you get rid of your "self", you become a divine being.

The Age Of Wonshibanbon

Wonshibanbon means to return to the origin, to the beginning. It means one returns to the master of all creations in heaven and earth; to the source of all creations in heaven and earth; to Truth, the origin of all creations in heaven and earth.

 The stars, the sun, the moon, the Earth, all creations and people in the Universe live lives of limited time.

For man to return to the origin, to the beginning, he must get rid of his attachments - his delusional body and mind, as well as the stars, sun, moon, and Earth. Then, only the origin, the empty space of the Universe remains.

 Returning to this Universe is *wonshibanbon* itself. When one is reborn as this Universe, he is the Soul and Spirit of the Universe, where the whole and the individual are one. Therefore, he lives in the land of heaven. *Wonshibanbon* is everyone returning to the origin and being resurrected as Truth, and the age of *wonshibanbon* is the time when the method to become this existence exists. It is now the age of *wonshibanbon* because *wonshibanbon* is happening at Maum Meditation.

The Work Of The Savior, Maitreya And Jungdoryung Is Salvation - To Teach The Method Of Salvation

People commonly believe that the Savior is someone who will come to the world riding on a cloud, and that he will take them to heaven if they have been devout followers of their religion. It is also commonly thought that they were simply chosen to live in this age of *Maitreya*, the *yonghwa* world (the world after the advent of the *Maitreya*) and that they will automatically become enlightened when the *Jungdoryung* comes.

But the Savior will make everyone cleanse their dirty bodies and minds, or in other words, wash away their unclean sins so that they can become one with the Creator and Truth. A person who has many sins will not be able cleanse them all, while a person who has cleansed all of his sins will go to eternal heaven.

The Wish Of All People Is To Live In Heaven

The reason we have religion and the reason we live, is to be born and live in eternal heaven. Most people living in the world would have had the following thought at least once:

If an omnipotent and omniscient God exists, he would have made man complete when he created the world, so that we would not have to live in pain and suffering and that we would live in a perfect world instead of this unjust one.

Although it may seem as though we live how we wish, by our own will, we actually live by the providence of God. Your life right now, the environment in which you are living, everything, is due to the will of the living God in the Universe.

Although there was no purposeful intention behind the creation of man, all creations and the world; it can also be said that because God is complete, everything was created so that as many people and creations as possible could be saved on this earth which is complete heaven and paradise.

In order to save as many people as possible, people will be harvested at a time when the human population density has reached its peak.

In the Bible, it says that man had sin from the moment Adam and Eve ate the fruit of good and evil. From the moment that man had the mind of discriminating between good and evil, he began to discern what 'goodness' and 'sin' are. This is the meaning behind "eating the fruit of good and evil".

While man and all creations are the children of God, having been created by God, man began to have sin from the moment he began to discriminate between good and evil.

We are able to live because the sun exists, and also because the stars, the moon and the Earth exist. Because of these celestial bodies, man's mind turned away from God and changed to a self-centered and selfish mind. A mind that is self-centered and selfish is trapped within itself and is dead.

In the Korean Declaration of Independence, dated March 1st, 1919, it was written that Korea had a population of around 20 million people. It became free from Japanese colonial rule in 1945, only for the Korean civil war, the national tragedy, to break out a mere five years later. After that miserable time, the population of North and South Korea combined grew to around 75 million people, less than a century later. During times of war, the population density always spikes sharply. When I was young, it was common for families to have more than eight children because so many of them died.

If people all had the mind of God from the beginning, there would have been no wars or human greed and the population would not have increased to this extent. They would not have felt the need to procreate because they would have been satisfied and the human species would have died out.

The world was made to be an unreasonable place so that man would sow his seeds widely, filling the world with people. This was in order for the Maker, Truth, to have a good "harvest".

Since this was the providence of the Creator, man was unable to become free from the comforts of his false body and mind or from making a living to survive. Man should now escape from that darkness, and become one with the will of the Creator and Truth.

Man can become Truth only when the existence of Truth comes as a human-being. While teaching this meditation, I found many people are foolish - they are happy when they are told that they can become Truth but they are not so pleased to discover that I, the person teaching them, am also Truth. They should know that if thousands of people have become Truth, then the teacher teaching them must also be Truth.

There is the saying, "Do you live to eat, or do you eat to live?" First and foremost, we live in order to become Truth; and this is the way we must live.

Now and in the ages past, our purpose, the purpose of mankind, was and is to become Truth in this age. This is the reason we eat and live. Those who live to eat are those who are dead.

I hope that the wish of all men will be fulfilled in this age when anyone can become Truth and go to heaven.

Living in eternal heaven is the wish of all people.

Religious Wars And Infighting

Ever since religions have existed in the world, there have also been never-ending religious wars. Not only do we still have religious wars, there are now also conflicts between members of the same religious group. If religions were perfect, the world would have already become one and religious wars would have disappeared.

I was invited to speak to a group of clergyman and during the lecture I told them the following: Man believes anything that does not agree with his own thoughts - his framework of mind - is wrong. In the same way, any religion that is not his own is believed to be a cult. However it is only when one is in a cult that he can have this kind of belief. People have no wisdom so they live without knowing what is right. There is no righteous person in the world so if man is to become righteous, that is, if he is to become a saint, he must repent all of his sins. Then he can become righteous - he can become the existence of Truth. How can a person who does not love his enemies be a righteous person? Man is unable to love his enemies; only a righteous person who has become Truth is able to do so.

I asked them how religions could come together in harmony when within one religion there are such deep divisions and denominations. I also told them that it would be natural for more denominations of each religion to keep forming in the future if people who have not become Truth continue to interpret their religious scriptures in their own way.

The clergymen all agreed that without becoming Truth, people will not be able to know Truth properly and will each believe that other religions are cults. I told them the way for religions to become one.

Even though there is only one Truth, expressed in different ways, people believe that they mean different things and each claims his own expression is correct.

 I then told them, the infinite Universe's great Soul and Spirit itself is Truth; and when everyone discards what he knows and discards his self that is a sinner by acknowledging that none other than himself is the greatest sinner, this great Soul and Spirit that is Truth remains.

If everybody is then born as this existence itself, they can become one in the land of Truth.

I told them that this is the solution for all religions to become one.

 To go beyond religion, to transcend religion, everyone must become complete, and when they do, all religious infighting and wars will come to an end. The way to transcend religion is for man to repent his original and actual sins and become resurrected by the Soul and Spirit of the infinite Creator and Truth. Then, religions, ideologies and philosophies can all become one. We can all live as one without conceptions of *your* country and *my* country and divisions between nations.

People See Outward Appearances
But Truth Sees The Inner Heart

In the Bible, it is said that people see outward appearances but Jehovah sees the inner heart. This means people judge others based on their appearance.

Man's mind is a bundle of attachments, therefore it is filled with self-centered and selfish minds. A person is judged to be a *good* person if he pretends to be nice, knowledgeable, great, modest, wealthy, well-mannered, and humble. Moreover, these days a person's worth is judged not by his heart but by external factors such as how much money he has, what car he drives, which house he lives in, and whether or not he wears designer clothes. But from Truth's point of view, there is nothing of value in man's filthy and evil body and mind.

A person of true value is one who has become Truth; a person who has become Truth is Truth and as such, he is complete.

A person doing the second level of the meditation can see the limitations of the consciousness of someone doing the first level of meditation. In the same way, when Truth sees a person who has done levels seven and eight, he can see the limitations of that person's consciousness - the areas he has not been able to become Truth itself and complete. Truth looks only at whether a person's mind has become the pure Energy and Light of Truth. This is what

Truth wishes people would become.

사람은 그 모양은 보나 진리는 그중심을 본다

People see outward appearances but Truth sees the inner heart.

The Noblest In The World

People live in a material world only, so they judge the value or worth of something simply by what they can see. For example, a person's value is judged by how much money he has and his position in society. However, such things are all futile illusions from a delusional world.

Man's mind is confined to delusions or illusions which he acquires while living in the world. What is the most noble, truly noble, is complete Truth itself, and a person who has become Truth.

The reason Truth has the highest value is that death does not exist for a person who has become Truth and he does not change. He lives in the eternal land of heaven. Human life in comparison to the time of the Universe is like a dream dreamt during a nap; and although man lives in this dream-like illusion, he is unaware that his life is a dream. Only Truth is immortal - eternal and without death - so a person who has become this existence is the most noble.

세상에서 가장 훌륭한것은 진리로 나서 진리나라 사는것

The noblest thing in the world is to be born as Truth and live in the land of Truth.

Kyuk-Am-Yu-Rok, A Korean Prophecy, Tells Us That At The End Of The World Only One Person In Every Hundred Leagues Will Live And The Bible Tells Us That Only Those Who Believe In God Will Live

People live from the energy that comes from the food they eat. When this energy disappears, they die.

It is possible for man to live forever without food, when he becomes Truth itself - when he becomes the very Energy and Light of Truth. If man changes his body and mind to the Energy and Light of Truth that never dies, he is Truth's Energy and Light. In other words, he is the Universe's Soul and Spirit, and therefore he will live forever even after his body disappears.

This meditation is about repenting the sins, the dirt, in one's mind in order to become the Energy and Light of the Universe. A person who has been absolved of all his sins is the Energy and Light of the Universe, so he lives eternally without dying. He is a person free from his conceptions and habits; a person of Truth.

This is what believing in God means, and only when one becomes this existence itself does he truly believe - only then does he truly, truly, have faith. It is difficult enough to become Truth and live as Truth, but man neither knows nor seeks Truth. Many die after being confined in a dream that they live in the world and those who live are few and far between.

People Are Dead Because They Are Not Truth - The Universe's Eternal Soul And Spirit That Is Energy And Light

Everyone living in the world is dead because people are tied to the conceptions and habits of their lives and to their shape and form.

Many people believe that they are living true lives and that they have not committed sins. But a person who believes that he is the worst person in the world is at least able to repent, and is therefore relatively wise. The people of the world live deluding themselves that they have not done wrong; that they are "good" and other people are "bad".

If one repents and takes a good look at himself, he will be able to discover that there is no one who is worse than he is. His self, a false delusion, has so many layers, he is unable to become one with the Creator of the Universe, the Energy and Light and he is therefore dead. Due to the fact that all people are dead, no one knows what it is to be alive. They know neither what death is nor what life is. It is natural that they do not know because they - their consciousnesses - are dead and not alive.

One can live only when he becomes the eternal and never-changing Energy and Light that is Truth. People do not know heaven and they live with the foolish belief that they will somehow get to heaven if they believe in it. But it is not possible to get to heaven unless one is reborn as the child of the Creator, because the world of the Creator is heaven and eternal life.

Only Truth, the Energy and Light of the Creator, can live forever. One must completely cleanse his unclean mind of illusions and be reborn as this existence itself. He cannot live forever unless he becomes this existence.

It is now the age of science, when it can be proven that things are exactly as they can be seen, just as they are. Things must be logical in order to be right. If one completely discards himself, only the Energy and Light of the Universe remains. Only one's self that has become Truth itself can live; it does not make sense to say that one can go to heaven just by believing in it. A person who has been born in the land of the Creator while he is living has this world of Truth within him even after he dies, which is why it is possible for him to live in that world.

Everyone is bound within himself, so there is no one who is alive.

Only a person who has become Truth is alive.

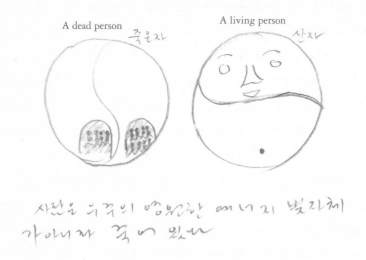

A dead person 죽은자

A living person 산자

사람은 우주의 영원한 에너지 빛자체
가아니까 죽어 있다

People are dead because they are not the eternal Energy and Light of the Universe.

Enlightenment Of Truth Comes
Only When One Discards

People commonly talk about having had an "epiphany" or having
been "enlightened" about something. However, enlightenment
means that one has become what he has realized and it only comes
along the way to Truth.

The Bible says that man was made to resemble God. This means
God is the very Soul and Spirit of the Universe - Energy and Light
itself. Man's mind would be this Energy and Light if he did not
have his individual mind of attachments. That man was made
to "resemble" this existence means that one is the same as this
existence, and to be the same is to be one.

It is to have no delusions within one's self, and to no longer have a
self thereby becoming this existence itself.

Enlightenment of Truth is to know Truth by becoming Truth.
One comes to know Truth as much as the demons, delusions, inside
him have been discarded, for exactly that much Truth enters in.
This is enlightenment. Put in another way, when one discards his
delusional conceptions and habits - his illusions - his consciousness
expands towards Truth. Enlightenment is what one comes to know
as his consciousness expands towards Truth.

God created the human mind to become one with God. When
one does not have delusional images inside him, only Truth remains

in his mind and his mind is clean. The more his mind expands, the more Truth is enlivened within him, what he realizes or comes to know at such times is enlightenment.

Man puts all sorts of different minds - everything he sees and hears - inside his mind while living in the world. Enlightenment does not come from putting something inside your mind. We have stuffed countless different things into our heads during our schooling and through religion, but enlightenment does not result from these actions. Only when one discards all of his conceptions and habits, can there be any enlightenment.

Enlightenment of Truth comes only when one discards.

Man Does Not Know Whether He Is Dead Or Alive

It is because man is dead that he does not realize that he is dead and not alive. He is dead because his self is a false illusion that is far from God.

A consciousness that is alive is when there is only Truth that is the great Universe's Soul and Spirit. Man is dead because of the delusions of his individual self. One can live when he changes his dead soul to the living Soul and Spirit of Truth. In other words, he must get rid of his dead self and be reborn as the living Soul and Spirit of Truth. This is resurrection, eternal life and the way to heaven.

Heaven is the world of Truth and the Creator. Jesus told us that there is no righteous person in the world, but the world of Truth is where only righteous people, those who have transformed into the Soul and Spirit of the Universe, Truth and Creator, can live.

This world is eternal and never-dying; it is the living land of Truth that is life itself.

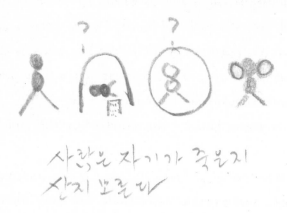

사랑은 자기가 죽은지
산지 모른다

Man does not know whether he is dead or alive.

Enlightenment

Enlightenment
is acknowledging with the mind;
accepting with the mind;
knowing with the mind.

It is what one comes to know - which happens to the extent he has become Truth - when his false minds disappear and his mind changes to the mind of Truth.

Truth emerges as much as one's individual delusional mind has been cleansed away and his mind has expanded, and what one comes to know or realize at such times is enlightenment. Enlightenment is what one comes to know when God enters his self-centered and narrow mind that is only as big as his form.

One's individual mind is the size of his shape and form. When it is discarded it becomes bigger and expands towards the great Universe.

Enlightenment is the realizations that come to him at such times.

A person who has become the infinite Universe itself is completely enlightened. He has become God,

and when he is reborn as an individual in such a state, his body and mind of Truth is the body and mind of the Universe. Therefore, he just lives, in the world of Truth.

A person who has completely become this existence receives a *seal* on his forehead by the Spirit of the Universe, and he has unfettered connection to the Universe itself. This is the seal of God.

When one can see that the origin of Truth - which is non-material - and the material are one, he has such a connection to the Universe, and this is the enlightenment of the whole body, or in other words, the body of light. A person whose delusions of his individual self have completely disappeared and exists completely as Truth itself, becomes enlightened that this state or this existence is perfection. Such a person does not have a mind of the past no matter how hard he tries to think that his body existed in the past. He does not die because he is the living Soul and Spirit - the Truth of the Universe - and for him, life and death have become one. His self that has become Truth, the Energy and Light of the Universe, lives forever. When one completely becomes Truth and totally forgets the past and his past self, he has achieved all enlightenments and he is complete. Such a person - who has become the Soul and Spirit of the Creator and Truth - has absolutely no minds whatsoever, and his mind is always at rest.

In other words, the mind of the Creator is not like the human mind which constantly changes; it is always of one mind. This is complete enlightenment, and it is this mind that can give salvation to sentient beings or *sattvas*. It is this mind that gives rise to all actions which result in the amassing of blessings in the land of Truth and a person who acts in such a way is completely enlightened. A person who does not act on his enlightenments is not enlightened.

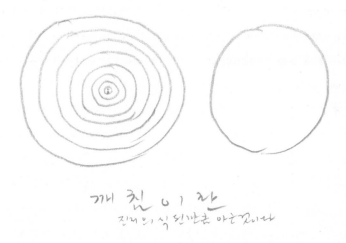

Enlightenment is what one comes to know, which happens only to the extent he has become the consciousness of Truth.

Faith

While people talk about being of the Christian faith, the Buddhist faith or having faith in other religions, it seems that they do not know the true criteria for faith. Does a person have faith if he regularly attends a temple, a church or a mosque? Or does he have faith if he reads the religious scriptures? Or then again, is faith having thoughts about the founder, the saint, of a particular religion such as *Shakyamuni* or Jesus Christ? What are the criteria for faith?

Without even knowing the criteria, we claim to have faith.

The word *faith* means to become one. To become one is to become that existence itself and the ultimate goal of all religions is to become Truth. When people say that they believe, it is their delusions that are speaking and they are simply just words.

True Faith

We come to truly believe in something when we can acknowledge it fully with our minds.

What we are certain of, what exists in our hearts, does not change. Therefore, we must believe something with our hearts, in order to say we truly believe something.

True faith is enlightenment. When one is enlightened, Truth that is the Creator exists in his mind and because he is this existence itself and he has become this existence itself, it is possible for him to have faith.

Faith is what one has in his mind, and he has as much in his mind as he has been enlightened and as much as he has become Truth.

Faith is one's mind becoming Truth itself;

faith is one's mind acknowledging and being certain;

and faith is enlightenment.

Faith in *Shakyamuni*, Jesus Christ and the other saints is to become *Shakyamuni*, Jesus Christ, and the other saints who are the existence of Truth. In order to become this existence, one must have enlightenment; that is, he must acknowledge this existence and be certain, and in doing so, host Truth in his mind. Such is what faith is.

It is said that if one has faith, he will go to heaven. This means if one has Truth inside him, he does not die because he is Truth itself, and as such he lives in the land of Truth; therefore he "goes" to heaven. There is another saying that the world is already enlightened, which means this world is the land of the Creator and Truth, and the land of the Creator is already complete.

Christianity tells us that Jesus Christ has already given salvation to all things. This means the Creator is originally complete, so therefore he has already given salvation to all creations in the world. Only people have to repent their sins in order to go to heaven because they are dead within their delusions. There is only one sin that exists in the world - the sin of not becoming one with Truth. In other words, one who does not or cannot become one with Truth is dead and therefore, he is a sinner.

If one believes in Christ who is God, it is possible to go to heaven and enter the land of the Lord.

Only when one's mind becomes one with God who is Truth, does he truly believe. Put in another way, one must be reborn as God who is Truth to have true faith, and only then can he be born and live in heaven - the complete land of God.

Having faith in Christ is to be reborn as God and Truth. Such a person is the mind of Truth itself, he is God and Truth, and therefore he is born in heaven and lives in heaven.

참 믿음이란
자기속에 진리있는 것이다

True faith is when one has Truth within him.

The True Meaning Of Not Being Able To See God Because He Is Light

Long ago, before I knew anything about Truth, a Christian told me that people cannot see God because God is Light and therefore too dazzling for human eyes. He also said that those who look upon the face of God will die.

I then asked him what use it was to die if we believe in God in order to see God, but he could not answer.

God is Truth that is the great Soul and Spirit of the Universe. God does not exist in man; man has only delusions inside him, which is why he cannot see God.

The reason people are not able to see God who is Light, or the reason the life of Truth is invisible to people, is they have never been to the land of Light. We can only really know Hawaii when we have been there, and in the same way, we must have been to the land of Light in order to see the land of Light.

Man cannot see the Energy and Light that is the great Soul and Spirit of the Universe because he lives a life that is focused on material things.

It is possible to see this Energy and Light when one has died. The land beyond one's death is the land of Light and it is Light itself.

When it is said that one will die if he looks upon God, it means that when one sees God that is Light, his self dies and only God remains. He then becomes God and is reborn as the child of God. Only a person who has become that Light itself can see the Light, and only a person who has died and has been born in the land of Light can see God that is Light.

Man is unable to see the Light; only a child of God - a person who has died and become the Light - can see the Light.

In the land of Light, the one God exists amidst absolute emptiness. This one God just exists everywhere. All creations in the world and the emptiness are the Universe's Soul and Spirit. They are Energy and Light and just oneness itself. A person who has been reborn as such, a person who has this existence within him, can see the Light and he has become the Light. Truth is this existence itself.

진리는 빛이라 보지 못한다.

People cannot see Truth because Truth is Light.

We Must Gain Eternal Life And Go To Heaven While We Are Living

We must gain eternal life and go to heaven while we are living.

It is illogical and nonsensical to believe in a heaven that one goes to after he is dead.

Material civilization has developed at such a fast pace that our lives have become infinitely more comfortable and more abundant than in the past.

However, man lives tied to his material reality and he depends solely on the words of religion, ideology and philosophy for spiritual matters. He is ignorant of the higher, more complete state of being - when such words actually become his, that is, when he becomes Truth by becoming complete in matters of spirituality. His conceptions and habits have become the absolute; he believes that what he does is right and that only his actions are correct. Thus, man lives as a slave to his conceptions and habits.

He does not know what heaven and hell are and he does not know whether he will truly live or die. There is no one who knows the fundamental principles of the world.

The principles of heaven and earth, or rather, the principles of Truth, are that the world and all creations are already complete. There is a Korean saying that one asks the way while he is already on the path, which means that one looks for something that is right under his nose. In the same way, while man is already living in heaven, heaven does not exist for him because he does not have heaven within him.

Man's consciousness has taken in or "eaten" so many different minds while living in the world. He lives as a slave to those minds because he has never discharged any of the waste. Even when we eat food, we must eat an appropriate amount and excrete out what we do not need. Man has "eaten" so many different shadows of his past without excreting any of it, and they are embedded in every single cell of his body.

Just as it is possible to clone a monkey from just one cell of its body, the cells of our bodies are made through the forms of our minds.

Man cannot know Truth because his entire body is filled with illusions, shadows. If he eliminates all of this falseness, only Truth remains. Truth is an existence that always just exists no matter how much you may try to discard or get rid of it.

Heaven exists inside one's mind when he has become Truth by transcending his conceptions and habits; when Truth becomes his self. If one does not become the existence of Truth, the Creator, while he is living, he cannot go to heaven.

Heaven is the land of Truth and the Creator. Man can become Truth when he discards all of his falseness and gives himself completely to the existence of Truth. When his self and Truth completely become one, heaven exists within him.

A person who has become Truth knows both that he has become Truth and that he has been born in heaven. He lives in the land of Truth that is heaven and he works for heaven so that he may have influence and rights there.

One lives in heaven only when he is in heaven while he is alive, and a person who has heaven while he is living, goes to heaven. Man cannot go to heaven because he does not have heaven within him. For a person who believes that he will go to heaven if he has faith, his definition of faith is wrong, and he cannot get there with such kind of faith. One must repent a hundred percent in order to be resurrected as a child of Truth and go to heaven.

One is being fooled if he believes that he will go to heaven after he dies - it is illogical.

Heaven is a world where only those who have been resurrected as the very Energy and Light that is the Creator and Truth can live.

One must go to eternal heaven while he is living.
For he who does not get there while he is alive, it is true death upon his death.

The Meaning Of Resurrection

We often use the word *resurrection* for many instances in the world that do not warrant it, such as when convicts take up a religion, when our minds become peaceful, or when we become devout practitioners of a religion.

Resurrection means that one has been reborn; and rebirth means one has been born again as Truth and he is no longer his past self.

True resurrection is the death of one's individual body and mind and his rebirth as the Soul and Spirit of the Creator.

거듭 난 나는 것을

To be resurrected

Man Has Thousands Of Delusions
And He Lives As A Slave To Those Delusional Illusions

There are many people living in the world but their minds are all different, with no two that are alike.

People have disagreements because everyone's minds and thoughts are different; this is the reason there are conflicts, wars, divorces and arguments about what is yours and what is mine. A person's mind comes from his very form and shape, which gave rise to the Korean saying, "he is showing the value or price of his form." This means that one's actions reveal the mind or value of his outward form. A person resembles his parents because his mind is born from the delusions of his parents' minds. Not only does he resemble them in appearance, his mind is similar to theirs as well.

Man lives according to this shape and form, and as he lives he forms his own mind. He is fooled into thinking that he is this mind that is formed. His mind becomes his conceptions and habits, and his mind is inherently rooted within himself. It expresses itself through the thoughts that arise when something happens. One's thoughts are one's mind, and as much minds as he has put inside him are expressed through a string, a clump, of incessant thoughts. These become the agonies, worries and heavy burdens with which man lives.

It was once said that around 70-80% of American citizens suffer from some sort of mental illness. The amount of agonies and thoughts one has multiplies exponentially when he tries to satisfy his desires while living in an ever-developing material civilization.

Man has lost his sense of priority because he has thousands of different delusional thoughts inside him and he lives as a slave to those delusional thoughts.

Born with the mind of his form that he receives from his parents, man then stores everything he sees and hears in his subconscious mind as he lives his life, such as his parents, friends, school and society. While this mind is a shadow of past illusions, he is fooled into believing that those illusions are him.

Even as you are reading this book, it is your mind that orders you to read, and your body that obeys. When the thought comes up in yourself that you must go somewhere, your body is put into action and it moves through that thought - your mind. For example, when you think that you must go to the bathroom, it is your mind that makes your body move.

The minds of shadows, of illusions, of self-centered attachments, are all illusions. A person who has taken in many such minds will live in an illusion to the extent of the minds that he has taken in; and he will suffer and be agonized to the same extent. All mental illnesses arise from these minds, these false delusions.

A Person Who Has Falseness In His Mind Lives A False Life While A Person Who Has Truth In His Mind Lives A True Life

Man is ignorant of what Truth is; he lives in a delusion following the conditions of the world, and in it, he does not know where he is going or what he is doing.

His mind only contains shadows, memories of his past, but these are false and not true. Namely, he lives with the mind of shadows. Because this mind is false, his life is also lived inside a false delusional dream. Just as one does not know that he is in a dream while he is dreaming, man does not realize that his delusional life is a dream.

Truth only exists once one has escaped from the false delusions. A person who has become Truth has cast off his self and lives as Truth. He has no self, and therefore he is without worries or delusional thoughts, and he is free and liberated. He does not have any false minds, so he is able to just live, which is a life of nature's flow.

Living a life of nature's flow is to live like nature, without any minds; to live with the mind of the Creator and great nature, as the salt and light of the world. Such a person has changed from a self-centered mind to a mind of the Soul and Spirit of the Universe - he is a person of wisdom and an eternal and indestructible person of Truth.

A life of nature's flow is a life lived by a person who has become Truth, and it is also the lives lived by all creations.

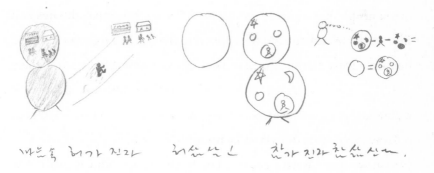

He who has falseness in his mind lives a false life, and he who has Truth lives a true life.

There Is No Righteous Person In The World

Jesus Christ told us that there is no righteous person in the world, including himself, and that only God is righteous. Just as he said, there is not and there has never been a righteous person among the people of the world.

No one has been able to become righteous because the method to become righteous did not exist. If such a method had existed, many people in the world would have already become righteous and this world would already be a world of Truth. If a righteous person had existed, a method to become righteous would exist, and there would be institutions and schools that teach people how to become righteous. A righteous person is a person of Truth, someone who has achieved "*dō*" as is described in Buddhism.

Achieving *dō* is to become Truth. A person who has become Truth is a righteous person so these two expressions have the same meaning. There is no school that teaches people how to become such a person.

One of the many clergymen who attended the seminars that were held in Europe said that going to heaven and gaining eternal life were things that could only be done by the grace of God. He said that these things could not be done by man no matter how hard he tries. This is certainly very true. Only Truth can make a person become Truth, and only Truth can take man to heaven, the world of

Truth. However, the person who spoke was waiting for the Truth of his conceptions, his images.

There are many people in the world who suffer from collective megalomania. In the strong framework of their minds, they believe that when Truth, the Savior of the world, comes to the world, they will be saved because they have the most faith in God.

What will Truth do when it comes to the world?

First, Truth will make man become Truth and give him birth in eternal heaven. The method to become Truth is the key to the kingdom of heaven. When it is said that one will go to heaven if he has faith in Truth, it means that those who have become Truth will go to heaven.

There is only one sin in the world. All those who do not become righteous are sinners. A sinner is sinful so he will end up dying and a righteous person is Truth so he will live eternally in heaven.

Teacher *Jung-san* told us that the Great *Dō* or Path that will make the world to become one will come from outside the current systems. This means that the Path will not come from existing religions. In the time of Christ, neither John the Baptist nor Christ came from within the Jewish religion. Just as the existing religions of the time did not accept Jesus Christ when he came, it would be the same if Truth came to the world today. People do not know the will of Truth and they are steeped inside the images of their fantasies.

When it is said that the Savior will come down from heaven

hidden by a cloud, it means that when he comes nobody will know. It is also said that he will be accompanied by trumpeting angels. This means that angels - those who have become Truth - will teach Truth to the people of the world.

It is said that the Savior will come from the sky or heaven, but the earth is also a part of the sky when seen from another star.

The sky or heaven is the original place of Truth and the Creator. A person who has been reborn as heaven or Truth itself is a person who has come from heaven or it can be said that such a person has "levitated" to heaven. This also explains the phrase in the Bible that says, a person of Truth will come among us just as Christ sent from heaven was among us. A person whose mind has been reborn as the mind of the Creator - the great Soul and Spirit of heaven - is a person of Truth who has come from heaven.

A while back, there was a church who claimed that they would be levitated to heaven. With over 500 journalists gathered, the church members awaited levitation, but it never happened. Around this time, many churches experienced a revival, with people who believed that the judgment day of the new Messiah had come.

The new Messiah is the existence of Truth, and a person who is Truth is the new Messiah. People do not understand the true meaning of the "new Messiah" and they are waiting for Christ from two thousand years ago to come down from heaven on a cloud. The great Holy Bible has been grossly misinterpreted. Christ was crucified by the existing religions of the time when he came to the world and told people that he was the Son of God. Even though he was truly the Son of God, they could only see his outward appearance; in their eyes, he was simply a Jew. Just as the Bible says, when Truth comes to the world people will only see outward appearances whereas Jehovah will be able to see the inner heart.

No one will recognize the existence of Truth when it comes because people view others through their conceptions and habits. This is why it is said in the Bible that this existence will come as a thief; that nobody but God the Father will know when he comes. It means people will not be able to recognize him because they are not Truth, and only the existence of Truth will know that he is Truth and that he is born in the world.

When it is said that thousands of people will see him coming down on a cloud, it means that thousands of people will see him and meet him, but no one will recognize him for who he truly is.

The person who saves the people of the world and makes them righteous is the Savior. As Christianity has told us, this is something that only the existence of Truth can do; if by the grace of this existence we are given the key to heaven - the method for all our sins to be absolved - then we must do so.

It is also said that the sheep will be separated from the goats. This means those who have less sins will be able to become clean and be reborn as Truth, "the sheep", but those who have many sins will not be able to escape from their minds of greed and attachments and will become "the goats".

If the existence of Truth, the judge, actually told people that they are goats or sheep, the goats would not leave him in peace.

When people are given the key to heaven, the judgment is whether they actually use the key to enter heaven. All people will be given fair judgment in this manner, but they will not know that they are being judged. Only a righteous person can make other people become righteous and only such a person can make the method to do so. A person becomes righteous if he discards his body and mind completely, becomes Truth, and is reborn as Truth.

Heaven is the land of Truth, and it is where only Truth - righteous people - live. When it is said that there is no one who is righteous, it means no one has been born in heaven.

세상에는 의인이 없다 진리인사가 와야만 의인이 난다

There is no righteous person in the world. Only when a person of Truth comes will righteous people be born.

Only Truth Can Teach Truth

People etch countless things into their minds through their surrounding circumstances. In other words, they live by "eating" or storing minds. Moreover, they want to possess anything that is advantageous to them. What they put into their minds become their "selves" and when something is in one's favor or when it agrees with their conceptions they believe that it is "right".

People are surprised to learn that none of these things are actually right. A complete person, who has become Truth and sees from the Creator's perspective, can know that everyone's words are lies and their actions are not done truly.

Whatever man says is a lie,
and whatever man does is false.
Only a true person who has become Truth speaks and acts truly.
The world was in an age when there was no Truth;
there can only be Truth when Truth comes to the world.

Religious scriptures are books that talk about Truth but in order to become Truth, Truth must come to the world for Truth to exist. When Truth, the Creator, created the world it was done with the intention of saving all things in the land of Truth - the land of Light. It was also created so that many people could live in the world of Truth.

The Earth was created according to the harmony and balance of the Universe. Just as there was a period of creation and a period of growth, there will also be a period of harvest. Many people think that people would not live with such suffering if the Creator or Truth is perfect. They also wonder why the Creator did not create man in a perfect and complete way, if the Creator is indeed omnipotent and omniscient. However, man is living according to the harmony and balance of Truth.

The countless stars in the sky also influence our lives. Man could not exist without the sun and moon and in the same way, all living creatures and micro-organisms live according to the great Creator's will. Through the balance of the Universe, the Creator made the human population increase in the period of growth that came after the period of creation, because it was a time of incompletion.

It can be seen in the Korean Declaration of Independence written in 1919 that there were 20 million people living in Korea. In the years since, there was the Korean civil war in 1950 and many people died. Not even a generation later, the population of North and South Korea grew to around 75 million people. People believe wars make the population decrease, but instead it multiplies because people give birth to more children during such times.

If people were created to be complete from the beginning, there would have been no conflicts. The human race may have already died out because people would have been complete; without feeling any want or lack, they would not have felt the need to have children. It is the unintended intention or will of the Creator to harvest as many people as possible by making them breed as much as possible. When you are gathering in the harvest, it is better to do so when the crop is as large as possible. All the scriptures are prophecies. They foretell the age of Truth and completion - that a world of complete people will come.

Heaven and paradise will become fulfilled here on earth, and it is here that people will live forever. This means that a person who has the world of the Creator, this place and earth, in his mind will not die and his Soul will live eternally.

Heaven is the place where only the Light and Energy of the Universe and Creator lives. A person who has become that Energy and Light will live forever.

Only Truth can teach Truth, and only Truth can make a person become Truth. Isn't this natural and logical? Isn't it nonsense to claim that a person who is not Truth could teach Truth? Just as the Universe created saints in times of need, someday the existence of Truth will come as a person and teach Truth.

Only this existence of Truth can make one become Truth and take him to the world of Truth. A person can teach only what he has in his mind; he can teach only what he knows. To know something is to have it in one's mind.

For example, a person would not be able to teach Uzbek, the language of Uzbekistan, if he does not "have" Uzbek in him. In the same way, a person cannot teach Truth or make someone become Truth if he does not have Truth.

While Truth has been spoken of by many people, only Truth can teach Truth and make people become Truth.

It is thought that in the world there have been many sages and people who have become Truth. What is important is the extent of their enlightenment. As the clergyman said, this is not something that can be achieved through one's own efforts, but it has to be given to him by the grace of Truth.

Just as Truth cannot be bred when the seed of Truth does not exist, one cannot teach Truth and make other people become Truth unless he himself is Truth.

If a person who had become Truth had previously existed in the world, the world would have already become complete. There would have been a method, and schools and educational institutions that teach people how to become Truth would exist. Moreover, the world would already have become one.

Truth and man are not separate but it is only when the existence of Truth appears as a human being that man and the world can be saved, and all people can live in the land of Truth.

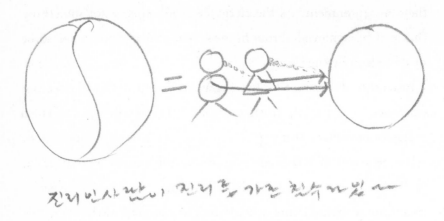

진리인사람이 진리를 가를 친수가 있다 ~

Only a person, who is Truth, can teach Truth.

Man Cannot See Truth -
Only A Person Who Is Truth Can See Truth

Truth is the Energy and Light, the *Jung* and *Shin*, of the infinite Universe. This is called *Sambhogakaya* and *Dharmakaya* in Buddhism, while in Christianity it is called Holy Spirit and Holy Father. These expressions refer to the body and mind of the Creator that created the Universe. They may seem to be different things but they refer to the same existence because there is only one existence of Truth.

The Creator that existed prior to the great Universe is omnipotent and omniscient, and it is what creates all things and gathers them back in.

The reason man cannot see Truth is he is unable to become one with Truth. He is filled with a selfish and self-centered mind which has blinded his inner eyes. This is the reason he cannot see. We must go to heaven in order to know heaven, in the same way that we can know what Russia is like only when we have actually been to Russia. A person who has not been to heaven can only speak from his conceptions; that is, he can only speak from the conception that exists in his mind.

One must become Truth in order to see and know Truth. Therefore, only a person who is Truth can know Truth. The existence of Truth can only be seen and known by a person who has become Truth itself.

In order to become one with the existence of Truth, one must discard himself and his delusional Universe. Then, only Truth remains and he can see and know Truth because he himself has become Truth or he has "been" to Truth.

The place beyond one's death, or the place where one's self does not exist at all, is the place of Truth. This is the place where one can become Truth. All those who have become such will live as Truth in the world of eternal and never-dying immortals.

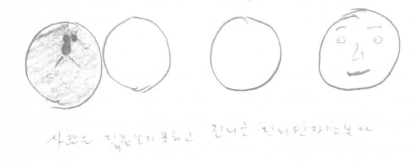

Man cannot see Truth and only those who have become Truth can see Truth.

One's Words And Actions Reflect
What And How Much He Has In His Mind

People live in the world with suffering and with countless agonizing thoughts and delusions.

Albert Camus compared human life to the toils of Sisyphus - that it is like having to repeatedly push a heavy boulder up a steep hill, only for it roll back down to its original position.

People claim to know things from inside their own self-centered minds formed by the environment in which they grew up. Within this mind, this mass of attachments, they say they know or do not know something.

People live, speak and act according to what and how much they hold in their minds. For example, people's professions and the ways in which they make a living is decided in this way. Those who have studied the law, or those who have law in their minds, make a living from the law while those who have studied medicine make a living from medicine. People live according to what they hold in their minds.

People's abilities also come from what they have in their minds. They move because they have minds and they live because they have minds.

People who do not have selfish minds are saints and complete people. It is not one's mind of attachments that allows him to live a good life. A person lives well when he does not have such attachments and he lives according to nature's flow.

A person who has Truth in his mind is Truth itself, and such a person does not live with a selfish mind. He can be said to live a good life, because he is free and he lives without worries, burdens and hindrances.

One's words and actions reflect what and how much he has in his mind.
A person of Truth speaks Truth and resurrects people from their graves.

Christians Say That We Can Only Be Saved By The Grace Of God

A person who bestows material or financial favors or aid is often described as being *gracious* or having *grace* but true grace is allowing one to spiritually become one with God.

God is Truth, and therefore one receives as much grace as he has cast off his delusions and become Truth. The highest grace one can possibly receive is being born in eternal heaven while living and living a life of that world.

A person in South America became very angry when I told people they can become the Creator and Christ if they repent all of their sins. He asked how a mere human could possibly dare to think of becoming the Creator.

The existence of Truth, the Creator of the Universe, existed from the beginning. This existence is the origin, and the mother and father of all creations and ourselves. When one returns to this origin, only Truth remains. When one returns to Truth and is resurrected as a child of Truth, he himself is Truth.

A dog begets a dog, a cow begets a cow, and a bird begets a bird. Therefore the child of Truth and God is also Truth and God.

How many people in the past died while searching and striving for Truth? Even now, there are countless people meditating and practicing asceticism in mountains and other places all over the world.

In the early days of Christianity, there was one group of Christians that practiced their religion through meditation and another group that practiced it in the form that we see today. The form of practice we commonly see today prevailed but there were many others who isolated themselves from people and the world in order to try and meet God. There are still many people who go to the mountains to pray or who take part in early morning prayers. This is like asking the way while standing on the path, and looking for Truth within Truth, because there is nowhere God is not present and there is nothing that is not God.

Only God can give us grace. The countless people who meditated, prayed, or practiced asceticism, were unable to receive God's grace because the time for God's grace had not yet come.

When it is said that only God can give us grace, it means only God who is Truth can make man become one with Truth. Grace is the absolution of one's sins and it is repentance.

When one denies his self by repenting, or rather, when he offers up his existence to Truth and only the existence of Truth remains, he can be resurrected as the existence of Truth itself. This is true grace.

All material things in the world eventually disappear but the existence that never disappears - the Universe before the Universe - is the Creator and Truth.

When one discards everything in the world, this existence

remains. When he is reborn as the Soul and Spirit of this existence, he lives forever and heaven is the place where he is. Do not seek God's grace within the framework of what you are already doing - you can receive it when you completely destroy and break down all of your false delusions and self. The existence who takes you to heaven through this method must surely be Truth. It is only natural that he can make people become Truth because he is Truth.

If a place where one can become Truth by repenting exists, it is, without a doubt, a signal that the advent of Truth has come. We must be awake at this time. Those who are too bound to their conceptions and habits will be unable to see or hear from within those conceptions and habits and they will have no desire to cast them off.

If one repents with the method of repentance, it is possible to receive grace.

True Wisdom

People who resolve difficult situations in a sensible manner are often described as being wise. However, the source of wisdom is knowing Truth.

To know Truth is to have become Truth. When one becomes the living God and Truth of the great Universe itself, and he has the wisdom of this existence within him, he will be enlightened of all things and know everything. Such a person is truly wise.

When one becomes free of his delusions - his point of view - and he has the viewpoint of Truth, the Spirit of Truth knows everything.

Such is a person with true wisdom.

찬 지 혜

True Wisdom

When we come to know or realize something while living in the world, we say that we have been "enlightened". But enlightenment and what man knows are two very different things; they are fundamentally different in nature.

What man knows is a realization about his daily life or something he did not know before. Enlightenment is what one comes to know and accept when he escapes from the conceptions and habits of his entity.

 There is enlightenment only when the individual that is trapped inside the narrow grave of his self comes closer to the consciousness of Truth.

 Put in a different way, when one's mind that is only as big as he is expands to the infinite Universe and he goes towards complete Truth, there is enlightenment.

 When there is nothing in the Universe, only Truth remains. There is enlightenment when all things have disappeared, or in other words, when one has cast off all his conceptions and habits.

When one denies even his self and eliminates all his images of the Universe, he becomes Truth. He goes towards Truth as much as his conceptions and habits have been broken. Therefore enlightenment only comes when one discards. Enlightenment does not come when one stores the words of saints he has seen and heard or when he tries to gain something.

The True Will Of Heaven

Heaven, or the sky, is Truth. The sky, or heaven, is the mother and father of all creation.

Heaven does not have a will or purpose, yet at the same time it does. This is the true will of heaven.

Heaven would not have any meaning if only the heaven of non-existence existed. Therefore, it is heaven's will to save all creations in the world of light. The heaven of Truth creates and saves everything without the mind that it does so. It can be said that everyone lives according to the silent will of heaven. Furthermore, when heaven comes as a person to the world by heaven's will, this existence will make people become heaven and live in heaven. These things are all the will of heaven.

When one sees from the viewpoint of heaven, all creations in the Universe are heaven and the sky. And as such, they are all alive.

Heaven has no beginning or end. Thus, a person who has become heaven does not die even if his individual self exists because his individual self has become one with heaven. A person who has become heaven is the master of the world. In the land of heaven, the whole world is alive except for man. Only man is dead because he has not become one with heaven, and a person who is heaven itself must come to the world to save mankind because heaven does not have meaning if man does not exist there. Heaven is alive in this way. The true will of heaven is to save people.

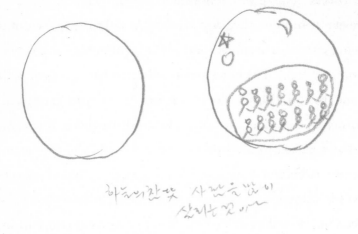

하늘의 참 뜻 사람을 많이
살리는 것이~

The true will of heaven is to save many people.

Heaven And Hell

Heaven is the land of the sky, and hell is the land of one's delusional hallucinations.

Heaven is the place where those who have become the Soul and Spirit of the infinite Universe that is oneness go. Hell is the place where one has made a self from the shadows of his past memories, and where this delusion lives - in false delusions that are not Truth.

Heaven is the world where those who become Truth live because they are Truth, and hell is the world that does not exist in reality.

A dream exists while one is dreaming, but when he wakes up he realizes it was not real. Living in an illusion, which like a dream seemingly exists and yet it does not, is hell.

It is death if a person goes to hell that does not exist after his body dies, while a person who has gone to the land of Truth is a person who is truly alive.

Heaven and Hell

Demons Or Mara

A demon is a person who has turned against Truth.

Even in heaven, there were demons that were not complete Truth. Our original mind is heaven but in the *sunchun* age - which literally means the age before heaven, or the age before Truth comes to the world - there were demons who lived only for themselves in that original mind. Status and differences in rank existed because of these demons.

The word *demon* is used to denote an evil existence. No one in the world wishes to meet a demon; on the contrary, most people are scared of demons. But what people believe to be demons do not actually exist in the current world. People should realize that a person who has not become Truth is a demon.

Very few people in the world believe they have lived wrongly; most people blame the world and other people. In actuality, nothing is the fault of other people or the world - everything is one's own fault because he is living wrongly. Those who know this are wise.

The worst person in the world is one's own self, who lives with the worst kind of mind - a self-centered mind. This mind leads him to believe others are right only when they behave in a way that suits him. This belief hurts everybody around him.

In other words, even though we are not aware of it, we cause harm to people because we behave in a delusional way. One's greed, his selfish mind, is the demon. No righteous person exists in the world; therefore all people in the world are demons.

A person who has become one with Truth lives with the mind of nature, according to the laws of nature. Therefore he is able to live a life of nature's flow. Demons are all those who live with a selfish perspective because of their minds of pictures acquired from living in the world.

Only a person who has been born as Truth is not a demon. The only sin that exists in the world is the sin of not becoming Truth.

If we knew that we were grotesque demons, we would not be able to hold our heads up for shame. We should all realize that a person who has not become Truth is a demon.

We should be resurrected as Truth as quickly as we can, and cast off our demon masks.

바위 라비어미러난

Demons or *mara*

Death

People believe death is when they stop breathing. Death is the disappearance of physical form and it is also when one does not have consciousness.

In the Bible, it is said that those who believe in Him who sent the son of God will not perish but have everlasting life.

He that sent the son of God is the existence of Truth, the Creator and origin of all creations in the world. All creations in the world are the children of Truth and are Truth themselves. Only man is unable to become Truth and therefore, death exists for man. In Buddhism, it is said life and death is one for those who achieve the way, for those who become Truth. This means neither life nor death exists and it has the same meaning as the Bible - those who have the existence of Truth itself in their minds do not die.

In the Universe, there is Energy and Light. This Energy and Light is Truth itself that created the Universe. It is the source that created the world. He who has returned to this source, the Creator, is born again as an individual with the land of the Universe's Energy and Light. He does not die because he is the Energy and Light of the Universe itself.

A person whose mind has been born as this existence itself has no death.

A person who has falseness within him will end up dying, while a person who has been resurrected as the Energy and Light of the Universe and Truth will live.

죽은 나란.

Death

Sin

The mind man has is sin. That is, not becoming one with Truth is sin.

The mind man has is the image of one's self - the silhouette or outline of his self. This self image is falseness itself.

A person who is false does not know he is false, and this is sin. To have sin means death. A person can live when he casts off his sins and is resurrected as Truth. We believe sin is breaking the Ten Commandments but true sin is not becoming Truth and this is the only sin there is.

Heaven is not a place where sinners live, it is a place where only those who are Truth live. Truth remains when one kills and eliminates his self, the sinner, and only those who have been born as Truth will live.

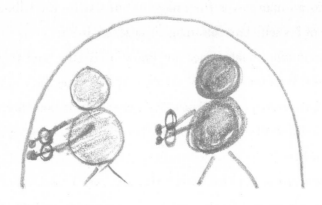

죄 간

Sin

People Who Live In Their Fantasies

All people in the world live inside the minds they have, a mind of their fantasies. They live without knowing why they live or where they will go after they die.

All people suffer and have heavy burdens but they believe they are the only ones who do because they are unable to see other people's suffering.

Man lives inside a dream of his fantasies, within the mind he has. Therefore he leads a dead life and he does not have any wisdom. A person who lives with a false mind of fantasies does not know he lives with this mind. Only when he discards his fantasies and is born as Truth, can he live as Truth.

Good And Evil

In the Bible, it says that Adam and Eve became sinners from the moment they ate the fruit of good and evil.

What man believes to be good and evil are self-made human conceptions. True good and evil is determined by whether one has become Truth.

A person of Truth is a true person; therefore he is "good".

A person of falseness is a false person; and therefore he is "evil".

The Second Advent And Levitation

The Bible says that the new Messiah will come on a cloud and that the faithful during the time of the end of the world will be levitated.

This means a person who has become Truth is heaven and Truth. If heaven becomes a person, he has "come" from heaven, and he who has become heaven has "gone" to heaven.

공중 재림나 휴거

The second advent and levitation

Only A Cult Calls Others Cults

There are innumerable religions in the world. Christianity alone has more than fifty thousand denominations. All religions claim other religions are cults. Which religion is the right one? Only Truth knows the answer.

A place where Truth really exists will not claim that other religions or organizations are cults because it will be a place that has a big or broad mind and therefore be accepting of everything. It will be a place that accepts everybody even if they are wrong.

People accuse each other of being cults because they are essentially the same. Anyone and anything that has not become Truth is a heretic and a cult.

Instead of being repentant of their selves which is truly the worst entity in the world, and the fact that they have the conception of a cult in their minds, people call other organizations cults based on their own perspectives, namely with only what they have seen and heard. Fortunately, Maum Meditation is simply a place where one discards his body and mind; a place where one discards and throws away his false self. Perhaps that is why no one thinks of Maum Meditation as a cult.

Now is not the time to blame others or call them cults; it is the time to repent one's self and become Truth so that all people can become one.

A Person Who Believes

A person who believes is a person who has become one with what he believes in. He is a person whose mind has become what he believes; a person who is the personification of what he believes. A person who believes is he who has the mind of what he believes in; he believes when his mind has become what he believes in.

Belief is not just saying that you believe; true belief is believing with your heart. A person who has become Truth is he who believes in Truth. He is able to always believe because the existence he believes has become his very self. You must believe with your heart, your mind, in order to say that you truly believe; merely saying that you believe is not true belief. Only a person who has done true repentance has true belief.

The Source Of Wisdom Is Knowing Truth

Wisdom is knowing what is proper and right. One has wisdom only when he has become Truth.

You may not understand or agree if you were told that from the perspective of Truth everything everyone in the world says and does is a lie. However, this is in fact true, because all people act from within their minds, from their own point of view. These actions are their perspective only - their words and actions are false because their minds are false.

A person who has become Truth itself is not fickle because he is Truth. He can be trusted eternally because his mind is the mind of oneness. On the other hand, man's mind changes at the drop of a hat, so it is impossible to trust what he says.

When one's mind becomes one with the mind of Truth, he sees and hears from the viewpoint of the principles of Truth. There is a world of difference between what he knows and what a false person knows. Such a person also knows that nothing is right or correct in the illusion that is human life.

When one becomes Truth, that exists of and by itself, there are no obstacles or hindrances and it is freedom without constraints. Everything in the world exists within one's self, and he is an eternal and never-dying immortal that has transformed into the Energy and Light of Truth where life and death do not exist. Therefore, he is the son of Truth, a divine being, an enlightened sage.

Man's mind is dead and does not know the principles of the world. As much as his consciousness grows, the more he comes to know; namely, when he discards his own consciousness and becomes the consciousness of God through the seven levels of Maum Meditation, he comes to have wisdom.

When one sees the world after he has become the Soul and Spirit of the Universe, there is nothing that he does not know; he comes to know everything, of and by himself.

People believe that wisdom can be found in books or in good speeches, but there is no wisdom unless one has cleansed his mind and has been resurrected as the Energy and Light of the Universe. Only God, the mind of the Creator, has wisdom.

If we do not become that mind, if we do not become God, all of our words and actions are false; they are just our illusions.

We must have the wisdom of God - the infinite light of the Universe.

When one's mind that is the size of his shape and form grows to become as big as the original consciousness of the infinite Universe, one's individual consciousness no longer exists and only Truth remains. Only at this time, or in other words, only when one has become clean and Truth alone remains, does wisdom appear. This is the reason becoming Truth is the source of wisdom.

진리를 아는 것 지혜 의 근본이나.
진리를 모르면 천지좋음모른다

If one does not know Truth, he does not know heaven either.
Knowing Truth is the source of wisdom.

The Reason No One Knows On Which Day
And In Which Hour The Lord Will Come

In the Bible it says that when Jesus was asked when the Messiah will come, he answered that no one knows, not even he, but only "the Father" or God knows. People in the world believe the form Jesus had two thousand years ago is the Messiah, and they are waiting for him to return.

Jesus is the existence of Truth. So if a person who is Truth comes to the world, he is Jesus. The eternal and never-changing Truth is the Energy and Light of the Universe; it is the existence that never disappears no matter how much it is eliminated; Truth is the eternal and never-dying God that existed before the world began and who will exist after the world ends. When this existence of Truth comes to the world, the Messiah has come. It is unrealistic to believe that Jesus Christ in the form that he had 2000 years ago will come down from heaven on a cloud. Truth is simply as one sees and hears, it is as things are. It goes against the principles of the world for a dead person to come back with the same flesh that he had in the past.

Among the people who seek *dō*, there are many who suffer from megalomania. They are people who want to master some kind of special ability so that they can boast about themselves. Truth is simply as one sees and hears, as things are. For example, the reason people cannot fly is they do not have wings. If there was a person who could fly, he would have already won all the Olympic gold medals.

The person who can fly the highest is the person who is the best at the high-jump; and the person who can fly the farthest is the person who is the best at the long-jump. If there was a person who could fly, he would have won all the medals for all short and long-distance track events.

People believe there are those who can fly, because they are foolish. A bird flies because it has wings, four-legged creatures crawl because they have four legs, and people walk because they have two legs.

Anything that has passed away does not return, and water that has flowed downwards does not flow back up. In the same way, a dead person cannot recover his flesh that has rotted away and this is Truth. If such a person does come back, he cannot be Truth.

A person can only speak of and teach people as much as he has in his mind. A person who foretells the coming of Truth can only tell such prophecies, and a person who has the Pakistani language in him will live speaking Pakistani. A person speaks, lives and teaches what he has in his mind.

Man only sees a person's outward appearance. He sees and judges others from within his mind of greed. Long ago, when Jesus Christ came to the world, the Jewish people did not recognize that he was Truth. If the existence of Truth came to the world now, people will just see another person and will not know that he is Truth, just as the Jewish people did not recognize Christ. There are millions of people in the world but it is impossible to know what they have in their minds. In the same way, when the existence of Truth comes, people will not recognize him because they will be unable to see the Truth that exists in his mind.

People are further unable to see or recognize him because Truth does not exist in their minds; their minds only hold falseness.

Only Truth can see Truth and only the living can recognize a person that is living. Therefore, man cannot see Truth because his consciousness is dead.

Christ told us that only the Father will know - this means people will not know when the existence of Truth has come because being dead, they will not be able to recognize him. Only the existence of Truth will know that he is Truth. Only he who is Truth will know when Truth has come, so therefore no one will know. It is again only a person who is Truth who will know when that day is, and in which hour.

The True Meaning Of The Second Advent

The Second Advent means to come again, and it also means to arrive again.

Truth is the great Soul and Spirit, the Energy and Light, that existed prior to the Universe. Christ was not his physical form. The existence of Truth - the existence that existed before Abraham - is Christ. This existence is Truth that existed before and after the beginning. Truth does not dwell in a particular man's form, so the arrival of the person of Truth is the second advent regardless of the form he has.

Everyone believes that he is his outer physical form. However when Teacher *Jung-san* said that he will come again, as did Christ and the founder of *Shim-in-dang*, they were talking about their inner heart, their mind, or in other words, a person of Truth.

Teacher *Jung-san* said that this existence will come from outside the system. This means he will not come from within existing religions. It is the second advent when a person of Truth has come but nobody will know it. People are waiting for the existence of their fantasies to come, but they do so from within the frames of their conceptions and they can only see outward appearances. Therefore they will not be able to see or hear when the existence of Truth has come. Being unable to see or hear Truth, and not knowing what Truth is, there is no way for people to recognize the person who has come again. Only a person who has repented by discarding himself completely will recognize him.

Only a person who has become Truth can know the existence of Truth; and one must search for that existence of Truth within his mind. Only when one's mind has become the biggest, the highest, the lowest, the widest and the cleanest mind can he recognize the advent of Truth. The second advent means that Truth will come bringing Truth with him. Since this cannot be found in a person's outer form, one must search for the person who has Truth.

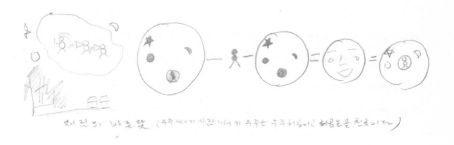

The true meaning of the second advent
(The Universe - people - the Universe = the Universal Emptiness. The Emptiness is Heaven.)

The Reason There Are
Countless Different Religious Denominations

There are innumerable denominations of each religion in the world. When someone within a religion interprets the scriptures in his own way, the religion splits and a new denomination is formed.

In Korea, there are many different denominations of Christianity and Buddhism. In America, Christianity alone has tens of thousands of denominations. When I lived in Korea, I used to believe Korean missionaries sent to foreign countries worked with the local people but I found as I traveled around the world that Korean missionaries mostly work with Korean immigrants or expatriates. The competition between churches and denominations is fierce due to the large number of churches and the limited number of Korean immigrants. Sometimes a few churches will come to an agreement among themselves to acknowledge each other as being legitimate, and automatically condemn new churches or organizations in their area as being false religions.

New denominations of a religion form when a person whose consciousness is dead interprets the religious scriptures in his own way - a new religion that is in line with his individual thoughts is then formed.

Religious scriptures are Truth, and as such, they can only be interpreted by a person who has become Truth. Man is unable to interpret them because Truth does not exist within his false mind. When the subject of religious scriptures came up during seminars, I asked many people if they knew the meaning of the religious scriptures but there was no one who truly knew. I understand the meaning of all religious scriptures even when I read or hear them for the first time because I have become the perspective of Truth.

New religious denominations will continue to form and multiply in the future because whenever something arises that does not suit a person's own conceptions, he leaves the organization and forms his own religion.

Each organization believes that others are false religions, and no one knows which one is the right one. Korean people are unable to unite because they belong to different religions and denominations and they do not acknowledge people who belong to an organization that is different from theirs. Jewish and Chinese people are much better at uniting among themselves but Korean people are unable to become one. Jewish people are better able to unite and become one because they believe in one religion.

If the spirits of Korean people were to unite, they would be able to become one even when they are scattered all around the world. This can happen only when people stop accusing other organizations and religions of being cults; when people acknowledge that they themselves do not know the true meaning of religious scriptures and admit that their own interpretations are wrong. All religions and all people will be able to become one when they discard their own thoughts and selves and acknowledge that they themselves are the worst people in the world. Truth will then emerge and they will be resurrected as the children of Truth who have transcended religion.

All interpretations of scriptures are nonsense because even though the scriptures themselves are true, no one has become the scriptures themselves. The problem is, people who are nonsensical do not realize that they are nonsensical.

One can understand the scriptures once he has become Truth by denying himself. He will be able to truly interpret the scriptures when he discards the wrongful thought that he is right, but furthermore, all people will become one.

Man dies after living one lifetime in the world. People propagate physically in a vertical line, but Truth propagates horizontally. It is eternal Truth that brings forth existence into existence; and it is Truth that existence of form is made into existing Truth.

Everything that exists in the world has a life-span in accordance with the conditions of nature. Even iron eventually disappears when it is melted and people's bodies die when you burn them. The bodies of all people living in the world have energy from the food they eat, and according to the conditions of nature their life-spans are decided by the limited number of cells they have.

However, a person who has become Truth - the Energy and Light of the Universe itself - has Energy and Light within him. Within Energy and Light, he is one with the Energy and Light even after his body dies because he is this existence. A person reborn as Energy and Light does not die; he becomes the eternal Soul and Spirit of the Universe and he lives eternally with the Energy and Light that is Truth. He does not live eternally with his physical body - he becomes the Energy and Light of the Universe that is the Soul and Spirit, and it is this Soul and Spirit in the same shape and form as his body that lives forever.

This Soul and Spirit is Truth that lives in the living land of Energy and Light and the whole world lives eternally in this place.

Before our bodies disappear, we must become Truth so that we may be born in the land of Energy and Light and live there. If we die before becoming Truth, it is death.

Man's body dies

The True Meaning Of The Soul And Spirit

We are told that we each have a soul that remains after we die, and many people believe this to be true.

The Creator of the infinite Universe consists of the Holy Ghost and Holy Spirit. This existence is the basic element of the Universe's origin and all things are the children of this Soul and Spirit. The land of Energy and Light, or the original land of the Creator, is a place where all creations in the world have been saved as Energy and Light, but only man is dead because he has not become one with this Energy and Light. When man discards falseness and becomes Truth, namely when he becomes this Energy and Light itself, the Universe will become complete. There is no one who can live without becoming resurrected as the Soul and Spirit which is Truth itself. All things that exist, the trees, mountains, water and creations, are Truth's Soul and Spirit and they have also all been born in heaven. But man is dead; he is trapped inside a grave that is his self because of his sins.

If one cannot unite with the Soul and Spirit which is Truth, he is on his way to hell and death. Hell is a place that does not exist; like a dream, it is an illusion. Living in an illusion is hell.

If man is compared to an onion, what remains when all layers of an onion have been peeled? The Universe will remain. The Universe must then be reborn as the onion.

Man is wrapped in thousands of times more layers of "self" than the layers of an onion. When he sheds all the layers of his delusional self that is wrapped around his mind, the Soul and Spirit of the Universe - Truth - remains. If this Soul and Spirit of the great Universe then becomes his self, his individual self becomes complete. He has a Soul and Spirit of Truth so he lives forever in the land of Truth.

What is believed to be man's soul is one's false self that has tens of thousands times more layers than an onion. This soul is not a true soul, so it is dead.

Whether one lives or dies depends on him becoming Truth.

We must all live, as the Soul and Spirit, the Energy and Light, of Truth.

False Soul   True Soul

The Day Of The Lord Will Come
Like A Thief In The Night

The Savior, who is Truth, can save mankind only when he comes in human form. Therefore, he will come to the world as a human being. *Jung-gam-rok*, a Korean book of prophecy, tells us the Savior will come as a person, and that he will come as a saint. The Bible says that he will come like a thief; that many will see his coming but no one will know on which day and hour he will come.

In the same way as things are at present, people who were around at the time of Jesus Christ, Shakyamuni, and other saints did not believe in them because the saints had the same human form as they did. When it is said no one will know when the Savior comes, it means that when a person comes no one will know he is Truth because they will not be able to see that he is Truth. This is the reason it is said the Savior will come riding on a cloud, or hidden by a cloud. When Truth comes as a person, many people will see him but no one will know that he is Truth. No matter how long people wait for a Savior from their fantasies, a Savior from their fixed conceptions, such an existence will never come. The Savior will come as a person but man cannot know Truth that exists within his mind. Hence, it is said that he will come like a thief, which means that no one will know he is Truth.

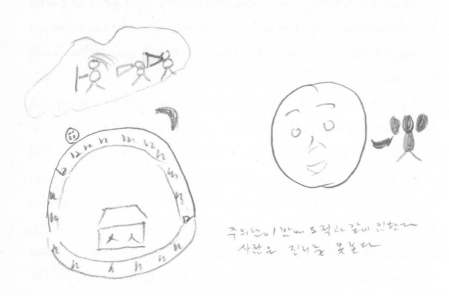

주의님이 밤에 도적나 같이 원한다
사람은 진리를 못본다

The Lord will come like a thief in the night. People are unable to see Truth.

The True Meaning Of Mankind's Salvation

People often believe that if they have blind faith, they will be able to go to heaven. There are also people who simply and blindly wait for the Savior because they believe that they have been chosen.

However there is no one who knows what the Savior will do when he comes.

The Savior will wash man's unclean sinful mind with the fastest and newest model washing-machine and make man's mind the same as his.

The mind of the Savior is the infinite Universe's great Soul and Spirit that is the Creator and Truth. He will resurrect man as this Soul and Spirit of Truth, so that he can live in the land of eternal and never-dying immortals. He will make man live as one without suffering and burden. He will wash their minds with lye so that they are no different from the material of the origin.

Kyuk-am-yu-rok told us to cleanse our minds by seeking a way to do so and the Buddhist scriptures told us to die a big death, a death without remains, or in other words, to die completely and reach Truth. It also told us that the time when this is possible is the era of *Maitreya*.

The Bible told us to make our minds pure, as if they have been washed with lye, and that a time will come when the sheep are separated from the goats.

All of the above mean that everyone must completely discard his sinful mind. Those who have many sins will find it difficult to become Truth, while those who do not have many sins will find it easier. Man's sins did not originally exist, but as his self-centered self with attachments formed, he was not able to become one with Truth. This is what sin is.

Man dies because man does not have Truth in his mind. Faith or belief is to have Truth in one's mind, and a person who has become Truth is a person who truly has faith.

The people of the world are all dead because they have no faith in Truth.

The salvation of mankind is when all people repent their sins and become resurrected as the Energy and Light of the Universe, the Creator, Truth and eternal immortal.

The Correct Meaning Of Wonshibanbon

Some people believe that the meaning of *wonshibanbon* is that we should go back to living the way we used to during primitive times.

The correct meaning of *wonshibanbon* is to return to the origin. It means we should go back to the place of Truth, which is the birthplace and the parents of all creation. This existence is Truth and the source of all creation; it is the place of the Creator; it is the place of life for us all and it is our original nature.

In this harsh world, people have forgotten their origin and live however they please. Leaving behind this age where people only speak their own words - lies - and returning to the birthplace of our minds, the birthplace of Truth where the spring of all life exists, is the true meaning of *wonshibanbon*.

When man has the consciousness of *wonshibanbon*, the consciousness of Truth, it is that consciousness - the Soul and Spirit - which will live. He will then know that the whole world is alive in the land of Truth and it will become a perfect world where all people live as one.

원시반본

Wonshibanbon - Returning to the origin

The Correct Meaning Of The Sound Of A Cow Lowing

Kyuk-am-yu-rok, a Korean book of prophecy, told us that when the end of the world comes we must find the place where we can hear the sound of a cow lowing. The Buddhist scriptures told us that man will go in search of a cow, find the cow, forget the cow, know that the land of resurrection exists and then walk the path of saving all sentient beings or *sattvas*.

It seems that both books used the word cow to represent Truth. The sound of a cow lowing is the place where words of Truth are spoken, and to seek a cow is to seek Truth.

A cow's lowing is a person of Truth speaking about Truth.

How To See, Know And Become God

Man cannot see the great Soul and Spirit, which is the Creator of the great Universe. This is because man lives with a mind that is only as big as his shape and form, and he lives behaving as this shape and form dictates. Therefore, just like a spool of string that has become tangled and misshapen, man lives so tightly tangled and bound to his self that he is unable to become one with this existence. Man cannot see God because his mind has become too stained.

The way of the world is that one knows, speaks, acts, and lives only as much as, and according to, what he has in his mind. Man cannot see or know God, and he cannot become resurrected by becoming one with God because he does not have God in his mind.

God is the great Soul and Spirit, or in other words, God is the body and mind of the infinite Universe.

One can see, know and become God when his mind becomes as big, wide, high and low as the infinite Universe; when his self has completely died and he has become the Universe itself.

신을 보고 알고 되는방법

How to see, know and become God.

The Formula To Save The World And Mankind

There is no scripture in the world that clearly tells us how mankind can be saved.

People blindly believe that if they keep faith with their religion, someone will come to save them one day, and that they will go to heaven. However heaven is not a place that is somewhere "out there". It is right here - heaven is inside your mind that has become Truth. Thus, if your mind is not reborn as the Creator and Truth, then neither heaven nor everlasting life exists for you. Only when one is Truth, does one live and only a person who has become Truth lives. The land of Truth or heaven exists only for a person who has been reborn as Truth and has entered that land. The Energy and Light of the Universe is Truth and only a person who is reborn as Energy and Light will be saved. In order to receive salvation, we must study and do the following:

Subtract man and all creations from the Universe. The resulting Universe or the emptiness is heaven.

If one is born as this existence, as Truth, one can know all worldly matters. This is the way to go to eternal heaven while one is living.

There is nothing more urgent in the world than becoming Truth.

There are many people who left during the middle of their practice of becoming Truth. They left to earn money and said they would return to meditate later when they are old. Each time, I told them that there is nothing more important than this, and that it is not too late to succeed in the world after they have become Truth. Many people found it difficult to return once they left, and there are some who died before they could come back. After they died, they may have realized that there was indeed nothing more urgent than becoming Truth. The source of true life decides whether one lives or dies and those who turned their backs on this source are all dead. My heart bleeds for them.

Those who have passed away did not have Truth and life, so they have ended up truly dying.

One cannot know what is truly important when he is too attached to his life in the world. It is most important to live, to truly live, in this age of living as Truth.

The formula for saving the world and mankind

The Source Of All Things Is Truth - All Creations Were Created Because Truth Is Existence, Not Non-Existence

The great Soul and Spirit, the Energy and Light of the great Universe, is the birthplace and master of all creations. It is an existence that exists just as it is, without a beginning or end. In the time before the coming of Truth this existence was described as non-existence. However, it is existent; it is existence. It consists of a Soul and Spirit and it is alive. It creates all things in the Universe and hence, it is called omnipotent. This existence is the one and only God, and it is the Creator.

People cannot see this existence and it is therefore ignored because of their unclean, sinful minds.

When one is able to see this existence, hear its words, namely when one has become this existence itself, he can live the life of this existence itself. Only this is life; the life of Truth. Completion happens when one returns to this existing entity; only then does he become a complete being who has achieved everything.

This existence itself is the eternal, indestructible and living immortal.

This existence is the Energy and Light of the Universe. All creations are this existence in form.

What does Truth look like? It looks like the whole of creation. All things are the embodiments of Truth.

The original Truth is the entity that exists of and by itself; the one and only God that exists amidst absolute emptiness. Only a person who has become Truth and is therefore alive can see Truth. Such an existence is the master, and the mother and father of all creations.

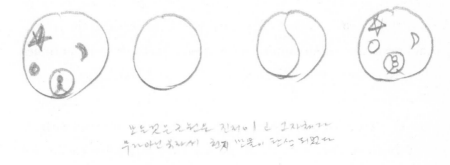

반드시 존재하는 진리이나 그 자리에서
무가 아닌 창조서 천지 만물이 탄생 되었다

The origin of all things is Truth. It gave birth to all creations in heaven and earth because it is existence, not non-existence.

One Does Not Have Any Human Minds Whatsoever When He Enters Into The Place Of Truth, Or In Other Words, When He Becomes The Jung And Shin Of The Creator

The Creator exists as the one God in the Universe, the emptiness, where absolutely nothing exists. The Creator is alive but it just exists, of and by itself. It existed before the beginning of the world and even after the world disappears it will still exist as the eternal and never-dying immortal. This existence is Truth so it continues to exist no matter how you get rid of it, or eliminate it; you may burn it or smash the sun, moon, stars, and Earth with an iron plank the size of the Universe itself, but it still remains. It exists without beginning or end; it exists of and by itself, and when conditions through nature's flow gave rise to cause, everything in the whole world was created within it.

Everything that exists in the world is the embodiment of this existence itself, and they are all just one. Only man is dead and unable to become one with God which is why he lives with suffering, burden, agonies and worries that arise unceasingly like bubbles in a boiling pot of porridge. If man gets rid of all of his delusional thoughts and his own self, he is resurrected as this existence itself. One's self that has become complete by becoming this existence has the mind of this existence. Therefore, he has absolutely no thoughts, no discrimination, and no human minds whatsoever.

God exists, and yet at the same time he does not have the mind that he exists. God's mind is the state of the emptiness itself, where absolutely everything has ceased. It is *Jung* and *Shin*, and when one becomes Truth and this *Jung* and *Shin* itself, he does not have the mind that he is this existence, nor does he have the mind that his existence ever existed.

One has no human minds at all when he is born as the body and mind of the Creator.

What It Means When It Is Said That
Something Is Holy Or Divine

When something out of the ordinary happens, it is often described as being holy or divine.

The word in Korean that means *holy* or *divine* is speaking of the Soul and Spirit - the existence of Truth. The two syllables of the Korean word literally stand for *Soul* and *Spirit* respectively. This existence created the whole world and it has the mystery of creation; such mysteriousness is described as being holy or divine. Therefore, when something is strange, out of the ordinary, or mysterious, this expression is used. There are many other words in the Korean language that originate from *dō*. The Korean euphemism for death literally meaning "to return" and a well-wishing greeting that means "to live well" are both such kinds of expressions, but there are many others.

신령스럽다는 뜻 신령이 만상을창조하니라

The meaning of "holy" or "divine" means God, the divine and holy, created all things.

The Universe Is Made Of A Body And Mind - A Great Soul And Spirit

The Creator, which is the master that created all things, is the body and mind, the Soul and Spirit, of the Universe.

All creations in the Universe came forth from this existence and they are the very image - the expressions - of this existence. The whole world is the Soul and Spirit of living Truth, and it has been this way since the beginning. All micro-organisms, plants and creatures are alive because they have energy. Just as people live from the energy of the food they eat, all creations live from the energy they have taken in.

All existing forms are the Energy and Light of the Universe, though they may have different traits and characteristics.

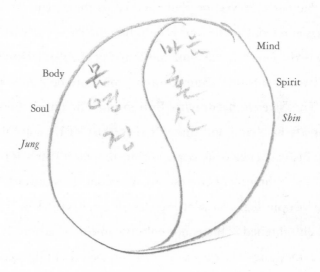

Body

Soul

Jung

Mind

Spirit

Shin

There Is Enlightenment
Only When One Goes Towards Truth

When a person's mind becomes bigger the mind of Truth enters into it. He has a realization that is equal to the extent the mind of Truth has entered his, and this is enlightenment.

Truth is the Creator, the Soul and Spirit of the great Universe. As much Truth as fills one's human mind, the more he comes to know Truth. This is enlightenment. Enlightenment only comes when one empties his mind and discards the entity of his self. When he does so, his existence disappears and in its place Truth appears. So therefore, enlightenment comes only when one goes towards Truth.

When people learn new things, they often say that they have become enlightened. This is not enlightenment, it is simply having learned something that they did not know before. Enlightenment is what Truth, life, knows in the moment that living Truth enters into a mind, a consciousness, that was previously dead. It is what one's own mind that has become Truth comes to know.

Coming From Outside The System

Teacher *Jung-san* told us that the existence of Truth will come from outside existing organizations and systems. This means the existence of Truth will not come from within pre-existing religious organizations.

Just as John the Baptist and Jesus Christ did not come from within the existing religions of the time, if the existence of Truth is to embrace all people, he cannot come from within one system. He will come from outside the system because if he comes from within a particular religion, he would only be able to save the people of that religion.

Furthermore, if he came from within a particular religion, there would be no way for all religions to unite, his ideology would be one that arises from his religion and the perfect ideology could not come forth.

This existence must come from outside the system in order that he can embrace all religions and enable all people to become one.

It Is Impossible To Know A Person
From His Outward Appearance

There are many, many people in the world. No one can know what a person's profession is, or what his personality is like just by looking at him. So naturally, it is impossible to know what his mind is like. It is a worldly conception that a sage or a person of Truth is a person who speaks as if he knows extraordinary things. There are some people who claim to be sages but a sage is a person who is Truth.

Jewish people judged Christ by his appearance and thought he was merely the son of a carpenter and not the son of God. Even now, they believe he was only a prophet and they are waiting for a Savior to come.

It is not possible to know if someone is Truth just by looking at his appearance. It is also impossible to know his consciousness. The only way to know him is to learn everything he has within him and become him.

If he is Truth, he will teach Truth and he will be able to teach as much as he has in his mind.

For example, a person who does not know Mongolian will not be able to teach someone how to speak Mongolian. In the same way, a person speaks and acts according to what he has in his mind. Although there are many people in the world, and there are countless more who have lived then passed away, the only person who can make people become Truth and go to heaven is Truth.

Even among people living in the world, those who live well and succeed are people who have constant and upright minds; people who have broad minds and can accept many things; and people who have positive mind-sets. If people become the mind of Truth, they will all work with this big and broad mind so everything will work out well for them. The Bible says people look at outward appearances while Jehovah looks into the inner heart. This means that people judge others based on their looks while Jehovah looks at how much one's mind has become Truth.

The Way To Become A Saint

I once read about four saints in an ethics textbook during elementary school. The four saints described in the book were Jesus Christ, *Shakyamuni*, Confucius, and Socrates. It said that these saints were in a sense still living because their words still remained in the world, and that these saints were the greatest among all people. At the time, I also wanted to become a saint.

There are countless people who searched for Truth in order to become saints, but passed away before succeeding. During discussions at seminars, there are many people who speak from their own conceptions. The question that is most asked is how I became enlightened and if it is really possible for other people to become Truth. They also say that the things I speak of can only be done by the existence of Truth.

The answer I give them is that I realized that I am Truth when I died and Truth remained. I tell them that I realized at this time that I had to teach Truth to the people of the world and that while teaching Truth and trying to raise people's consciousness to the same level as mine, I became enlightened of the method to go towards Truth. I also tell them that many people have already become complete. I also tell them that the existence of Truth is a person who has Truth, not a person of their fantasies and delusions. I ask them to discard this existence in their minds and change their conceptions.

I ask people, if a person teaches Truth and successfully makes people become Truth then isn't the teacher himself Truth? Everyone agrees when it is put in this way.

In my childhood I used to wonder if there was a school that teaches people how to become saints. I have made such a school and many people are becoming saints.

Abilities Such As Being Able To See And Hear With The
Eyes And Ears Of Heaven, Walk With The Legs Of God,
Know About Past Lifetimes, Know That The Cycle Of
Death And Rebirth Is Over, Know Other People's Minds,
And Other Such Abilities Come When One Becomes
Truth

The sky that we can all see is Truth and the Creator. The ability
to see with the eyes of heaven is seeing things not from one's own
individual perspective but seeing things from the perspective of
the sky which is Truth, or rather, having become the sky. What one
hears after one has become the sky is the ability to hear with the ears
of heaven. Likewise one knows the cycle of death and rebirth is over
when he completely disappears and he becomes Truth. All other
abilities of this kind, such as the ability to walk with the legs of
God and know other people's minds, come when he becomes Truth
and heaven.

In the early days of this meditation, I enabled many people to
receive the spiritual ability to see the real world. Because it was
their spirits that saw and heard this world, it can be said that this
ability was in essence all other abilities listed above as well. When
one becomes heaven that is Truth, he receives all of these abilities
and this itself means he has become complete and Truth itself. Only
when one has become Truth itself, can he be said to truly have the

ability to see and hear with the eyes and ears of heaven.

However no one had true spiritual abilities, so after awhile what they saw was nonsense because they started to see the expressions of their own minds. The abilities of anyone whose mind has not become complete are false.

The only person with true abilities is a person who has become heaven and Truth. Because such a person is heaven itself, everything that he sees and hears in the world having become heaven is also heaven. Therefore, it can be said that he has received all possible abilities. A person who has become Truth has the wisdom of Truth; and this is what all abilities are.

Why Illnesses Become Cured

Teacher *Jung-San* told us that in the future when people have become Truth, the first ability they will gain will be the ability to cure illnesses. Man is trapped inside the framework of what he believes to be his self, and he is tied up with countless minds. When the minds and habits inside his body disappear on his way towards Truth, the blocked energy channels in his body begin to flow freely. This enables him to recover from his physical illnesses because the human body and mind are not separate but one. They disappear because he becomes free from the karma and habits that had bound him and when this happens, Truth dwells within him and allows the energy channels in his body to flow according to the natural order of the Universe and Truth.

Everyone who has done this meditation has experienced an improvement in their health. Initially they had countless minds inside them because of the consciousness they had, and when these disappeared, they all experienced an improvement in the function of some parts of their bodies. It is possible to live to a ripe old age if one does not hold anything in his mind. The life-span of heaven is the age of heaven itself, so those who have done this meditation will be able to live long and healthy lives.

It is believed that a person who does *dō* will gain powers such as being able to fly, cure all illnesses, and other such supernatural abilities but the abilities people think they will gain are just human delusions. Just as there are still people who believe that such things can happen, there are some who have fantastical delusions and believe that a dead person's flesh will regenerate so that he can come back to the world. The way of the world is that things are just as you see it and hear it - just as things are. All material things have life-spans according to the conditions of the world and when they disappear from the world they never return. This is the way of the world and Truth. If Truth comes in such a way - by returning from the dead - then such a person is not Truth. If something exists in the world, it exists because it exists in the world at present.

The Age Of Becoming Maitreyas

A disciple of *Won* Buddhism asked the founder *So-tae-san* when the *Maitreya* will come, and he was told that he will come soon. He also said that in this age, everyone will all become *Maitreyas*. When asked if there is a person who has already become so, he replied that everyone who becomes enlightened are *Maitreyas*.

Maitreya is the complete existence, and the existence of Truth. The existence of *Maitreya* will become enlightened of the way to make others become like him and make all people become one. When this happens and people change, it is the fulfillment of the *yong-hwa* world - a perfect world.

A Person Must Be Truth In Order To Teach Truth

The countless different religious sects and denominations in the world all claim that Truth exists within their organization and that their religion is right. However people do not actually know what is right because they do not have wisdom; instead, they insist that their religion is the right one. Ultimately, conflicts arise because a perfect or complete organization does not exist. If it had existed, religions would not have split into so many different sects and denominations because everyone would have joined it.

A place that is true and complete has to be a place that enables people to become the existence of Truth itself.

We believe there have been numerous enlightened people in the world, and many people have spoken as though they know Truth. However, if these people had been truly enlightened, a method for other people to become so would exist, and an organization where that method is taught would also exist. People who we believe have been enlightened were only enlightened to a certain extent, and the level of their enlightenment varied from person to person.

In Maum Meditation, it can be said that a person has been "enlightened" even after the first and second level. However true enlightenment is when one has become Truth itself - when one's past self no longer exists.

If a method had existed, everyone would already have become

enlightened, and the world would have become one. Everyone would already be living in paradise, and the world would have become a peaceful place.

If there had been an enlightened person who taught people how to become like him, such a place would presently exist. But as far as I know, there is no such place anywhere in the world at the moment.

People blindly believe anything they are told, the words of any ghost, as being the words of enlightenment; but if you ask anybody who has completed the meditation if there had been any enlightened person in the world, they all reply in the negative.

A method that enables man to become complete now exists in the world because over the last eight years, I was enlightened of such a method, or more precisely, the methods of the eight levels of meditation.

There was not one person who successfully achieved these levels on their own no matter how hard they tried. The methods of each level must be taught and guided for a person to be able to achieve them. If a method does not exist, it is impossible to get to the place of Truth.

It is said in the Bible that such an end can only be achieved through the grace of God, and this is indeed true. A person can teach only as much as what he holds in his mind, therefore only the existence of Truth can teach Truth.

Insane People

People in the world all look as if they are normal but in fact they are all insane. Because of their minds of attachments and greed, they live with delusional minds of falseness and attachment - the shadows of past memories.

We believe that a person who mumbles to himself is insane while a person who is silent is not. However, if there are illusions inside a person and delusional thoughts continuously arise in his mind, those illusions are the driving force behind his actions and such a person is insane. In order to become a sane person, one must be reborn as his original consciousness, as Truth. There is not one person in the world who is sane. Only a righteous person who has become true is sane.

The Greatest Person In The World

There are many great people in the world but they are only great in their own conceptions and habits - there is no one who is truly great.

The greatest person in the world is a person who has become Truth. He is great because Truth is perfect. In Korean, the word *great* literally means to be "well-born". A person who has been born as Truth is the true meaning of the Korean words for *great* and *good-looking*. The greeting, "live well" means one should live as Truth.

The Korean book of prophecy *Kyuk-am-yu-rok* entreats us to be born as Truth in the age of Truth. A wise person is one who becomes Truth. He is great because he knows the ways of the world and lives properly. The difference between those who have become Truth and those who have not is the difference between normal and abnormal people.

Truth

Truth is the existence that never changes, and it is life itself. Not only did it create all things in the world, it is the master of all creations. This existence is the Universe that existed prior to the current Universe; it is the existence that created it. It is the great Soul and Spirit of the Universe.

It is  this existence.

Truth: the Soul and Spirit of the infinite Universe

In Taoism, this existence was called *dō* or *tao*, and in Christianity, it was called God, and in Buddhism, Buddha. It is also called Allah, and in Korea it is called *Haneol-nim*. Other names such as original nature, the origin, the Creator, one's true self, all refer to this existence of Truth. People have given this existence various different names.

This existence is the body and mind of the Universe and it is called *Jung* and *Shin*, *Sambhogakaya* and *Dharmakaya*, the Holy Spirit and Holy Father, and Energy and Light. It is also called Soul and Spirit. These are the names for *yin* and *yang* - the origin of Truth.

The Correct Meaning Of Savior

A Savior is the entity that saves the world.

In order to save the world, he must get rid of heaven, earth and man, return them to the place of Truth and the Creator, and enable them to become reborn as this existence of Truth. The person who does this is the Savior. The entity that saves all creations in the world is the Savior.

He will enable all creations in the world to be resurrected as the Energy and Light of the Universe, which is Truth and the Creator. And by doing so, he will enable them to live in that land of Truth. The Savior is the person who does these things.

No Matter How Hurriedly He Travels,
Man Has Nowhere To Go

The people of the world live and move according to the visions of their delusions. Their delusional visions cause their suffering and because they live as their visions order them to live, they are uselessly busy without achieving anything. Furthermore, it is not possible for them to achieve anything.

When they are asked to become Truth, it seems they are unable to hear clearly because they either do not understand what this means or they say they are very busy. But don't we manage to fit in activities we really want to do, such as hiking or fishing, even when we are busy with work?

It is when there is limited time that people usually manage to get things done, such as running errands, hiking, or meeting old friends. When we actually do get a long break, we achieve less.

No matter how busy a person is, is there anything more urgent than finding oneself, becoming complete so that one becomes eternal and imperishable?

The things that keep us busy do not result in any actual achievements even when we think they do - it is a delusion, an illusion, that busily runs around in those activities.

I often see that those who have the right mind-sets seek Truth no matter how busy they are, and many of them achieve Truth. Instead of being needlessly busy without anywhere to go, shouldn't you strive towards eternal life and heaven?

Only when God exists within one's self, can one ask God questions and receive answers. Revelations from God are the answers that one receives from God who exists within him. It is through wisdom that one hears and understands the words of God.

God does not tell us to do this or that through words; it is through wisdom that we can understand what God is saying.

When a person who has not become Truth claims to have heard the voice of God, he has only heard the voices of his own delusions. Anyone who has completed levels seven and eight of this meditation can hear God's voice through wisdom. If one asks why we live, God answers that we live because we live; and if one asks what the objective of life is, he answers that it is for man to become complete and live forever. Again, these answers are understood through wisdom.

One can also know through wisdom that the end of the world is only the end for those who are dead, while it signals the beginning of a new world for those who are living.

If one asks God how man can become one of the living, he would reply that man will be able to live if he offers up all of his self-centered body and mind that is obsessed and attached to himself.

If asked why man was not made complete from the beginning, God would answer that if that had been the case the population would not have grown as much. This would also be understood through wisdom. Man was made the way he was, so that the human population would multiply as much as possible during the period of growth, and so that in this period of harvest, there would be as many people as possible to "harvest" in the land of Truth.

Maum Meditation Is The Practice Of Discarding One's Self, And Discarding Only

Although everyone in the world believes that he lives in the world through his own merits, everyone lives by the providence of God. In Korea, there is a saying that a person credits his successes to his own greatness while blaming his ancestors for his failures.

No one in the world knows that they are living wrongly. Everyone believes that they themselves are in the right and faults or mistakes are only made by those around them. This is the reason people blame others.

Stop blaming others - know that you have done wrong and therefore, you are the one at fault. Other people's faults exist because the fault itself exists in your mind. For example, the people you dislike exist because hate exists in your mind. It is the same with enemies, *good*, and *great* people; they all exist because these things exist in your mind. Whether you live well or poorly, succeed or fail, these things all happen because they exist inside your mind. Everyone in the world should throw away these minds, discard even their bodies, become Truth and live as Truth. This is what people at Maum Meditation are doing. Discarding one's body and mind, and only this, is the practice of Maum Meditation. What need is there to judge whether something is a cult or heretical when one is discarding and getting rid of his self?

When one becomes the existence of Truth, he is reborn and lives in eternal heaven, and this is the practice of Maum Meditation.

The Definition Of What Is And Is Not A Cult

The difference is that of right and wrong.

The difference is that of being correct or incorrect.

It is also the difference between Truth and what is not Truth.

The difference between right and wrong, being correct and incorrect, and that which is Truth and not Truth, is that the former is true and the latter is false.

That which is true is Truth and that which is false is not Truth. It is also possible to discern what Truth is in the following way: an organization where one only listens to words of Truth is not Truth because one does not become Truth. Truth is only Truth when it is 100% Truth. Anyone that has not become 100% Truth is completely false.

In that case, only the place where one can become Truth completely is not a cult. Only a person who lives his life carrying out actions of Truth, that is, only a person who lives for others and saves the world through the will of Truth, is not a heretic or a cult member.

Man must first gain true consciousness if mankind is to live and do well.

The true consciousness is the mind of God, which is righteous. The more human civilization develops materially, the more developed a country becomes, the higher the incidents of crime, drug use, and suicide. Sweden and Denmark, arguably two countries in the world with the highest quality of life, have the highest rates of suicide in the world.

The results of a happiness index showed that generally less developed countries received higher scores for happiness. Those whose minds hold a lot of falseness chase false things until they eventually die. When people come to their 'original senses' or rather, when they become the original mind, people are less busy. This is because even while they work, they do so with a secure mind - the mind of oneness. Therefore, they are able to work without stress or difficulties because they do not have human minds.

Many people from Communist societies in the past were dedicated to the Communist ideology in order to receive recognition. Only later, after they received awards and decorations, did they realize that these accolades are meaningless. Living for others is a true accolade that never changes or loses its luster.

A person who has come to his true senses and has become Truth will live for others.

If all of mankind discards their selves and lives resurrected as Truth, all people will live a life of one, a life of caring for others. This is the way for all mankind to live well.

Even When They Are Told Again And Again, People Do Not Understand

Since I started spreading Truth in the world, my message has always been the same: the Universe is one, as is existence and non-existence. All things are already complete but only man does not know oneness because his consciousness is dead.

I also tell them that the world was created by the Universe before the Universe. This existence itself is the everlasting and never-changing Truth and it is alive. The place that man reaches when man dies and transcends himself is the Creator's land which is Truth. Only those who have died can become Truth and furthermore, man must become complete in order for the world to also become complete.

However, no one understands what I tell them, even when they have been told many times.

I have told them the above message for the past eight years, but only now that some have achieved full enlightenment do they say that they finally understand, and that they have also been enlightened to the same. However, when I do not tell them something explicitly because I take for granted that they will know it, I find that they do not actually know.

People listened only to the sounds of the words I spoke, from within the framework of their conceptions with calculating heads of vipers. They were not able to hear the words with minds of Truth.

Only when their minds become that of Truth do they finally understand; it is the mind of Truth that understands. Until now, I felt like I was speaking to people with metal ears. In the early days of spreading Truth, I spent many nights drinking and borrowing the alcohol's strength to tell them stories of Truth. But it was like reading scriptures to ears of metal.

People only understand as much as they already hold in their minds. And just as they live their lives according to what their minds hold, as much Truth as they have in their minds, they understand exactly that much. Even those who have been enlightened say that they become more enlightened daily as they listen to my words that I have repeated many times in the past. Enlightenment is what one's mind comes to know and becomes certain of. It also shows how much he has gone towards Truth.

A person who has been completely enlightened will completely forget his past self. This is what it is to completely become Truth.

People Who Beg For Blessings

It seems people believe in religions because they have certain agendas.

When I ran a college preparatory tuition school in *Daegu*, I went hiking every day. Students would come in the afternoons, so I would use my free time in the morning to go hiking.

At the top of the mountain, which could only be reached by climbing hundreds of steps, there was a statue of a Buddha carved into a huge rock. Every day I saw an endless stream of people come and pray for various blessings, such as college admittance for their children, business success, or wealth. Once in a while I would sit behind the carving to meditate and on one such day when my eyes were closed, I found that I became one with the carving. From its viewpoint, I could see that there was no one worthy of receiving blessings. There was no room in their minds for blessings to enter. It is the same in churches and all other religions: all people believe in religions while wishing for something in return.

People live according to what they hold in their minds. This determines the size of one's mind, which is sometimes described as one's 'plate' in Korean. The way people live is determined by the size of their 'plate'.

People may ask for blessings, but the existence that is God and Buddha is not an entity that listens to such pleadings. One's delusions are begging to a false delusion and this only adds to his karma of greed.

Truth is not an existence that grants blessings which benefit people's delusional individual lives. Whether one lives well or poorly depends on how much he has opened his mind. People should focus on increasing the size of their minds. When people live with big minds - the mind of Truth - everyone will be able to live well.

Where Is Heaven And Where Is The Land Of Truth?

We see the sky outside every day. The sky is Truth and what religions call the absolute.

But people cannot truly see the sky. This is because they do not have the sky in their minds. A sky that does not exist in your mind is not your sky; and you cannot know it, because you are not the sky.

A person who has the sky, Truth, within him, is himself the sky - an eternal and never-dying immortal. He has become immortal.

Man can know the sky only when it exists within him. It only exists when he disappears and becomes the sky itself. It is the same for the land of Truth - only when the sky exists within man, is there a heaven. The land of the sky is heaven and the land of Truth.

A person who has the sky within him is a person who lives in eternal heaven.

When Man Becomes The Master Of The Universe, The Age Of Man Begins And The World Becomes Complete

The Soul of the Universe is without beginning or end, and it consists of a Soul and Spirit. Its life span is also without beginning or end. All creations and man were created in a complete state by this existence that is the Creator but man could not become one with this existence of Truth because of his self-centered mind. If one's self-centered illusionary body and mind are completely eliminated, only the Creator that is Truth remains. If then, one is reborn as the Energy and Light of this Creator, this place right here becomes heaven and eternal life.

Namely, one's own heaven is constructed.

He himself is the master, and he constructs his world which he lives with forever. The earth and heaven are one; this earth, here, becomes heaven inside one's mind that has become Truth. It is the age of man because man is the master and it is when man lives that everything in the world becomes complete.

Gold Is Gold Only When It Is A Hundred Percent Gold

If something is 99% gold mixed with 1% silver, it cannot be called gold. It should be called gold that is mixed with 1% silver. It is the same for Truth and falseness - something is either false, or it is true. It is either Truth or it is not. In levels seven and eight, when one receives the seal of Truth, when one's individual self becomes the great Soul and Spirit of the Universe itself, when one becomes enlightened that his individual self has become complete, he becomes pure "gold". Anyone who has not been enlightened of such has not become Truth - he is false Truth.

The Way For Mankind To Become One, And For All Religions, Philosophies And Ideologies To Become One

In the world, there are endless wars between nations, religious wars and religious infighting. There are ideological conflicts because everyone's thoughts are different, and in philosophy everyone's opinions differ also.

Mankind makes enemies of those whose opinions differ from theirs and they fight until there is a winner. This happens because man does not know what it is to be complete; he only knows his own point of view. The way for all wars to cease, the way for mankind to become one and for all religions, philosophies and ideologies to become one is for all people to be resurrected with the complete consciousness of Truth. If all people become complete, they may all have different shapes and forms but they will become one because they will be of one mind. Moreover, religions, philosophies and ideologies will become one because instead of being viewed from one's individual standpoint, they will be viewed from the standpoint of Truth that is complete.

What "I Am The Way, Truth And Life, And No One Can Enter Heaven Without Going Through Me" Means

The master is one's original nature, also called the Creator and Truth, which exists within himself. One's mind going towards the Creator, who is Truth and the absolute God of the Universe, is the Way, Truth and Life. This is all that a person of Truth looks at; he does not look at a person's appearance but at whether his mind has become Truth. Without going through this existence, no one can go to heaven.

Most people believe that the Way, Truth, and Life is a certain shape and form, but it is actually the existence of Truth and the Creator. Without becoming this very existence - without becoming Truth - no one can go to heaven.

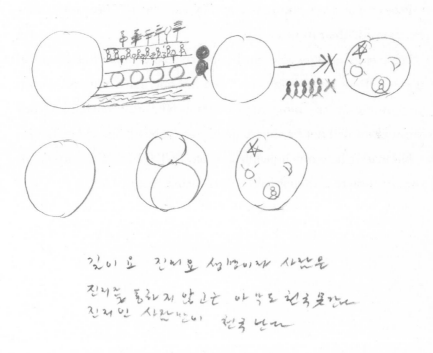

길이요 진리요 생명이라 사람은
진리를 통하지 않고는 아무도 천국못간다
진리인 사람만이 천국 간다

"I am the Way, the Truth, and the Life" means man cannot get to heaven without going through Truth. Only those who are Truth will be born in heaven.

Even Though They Have Eyes And Ears, People Cannot See Or Hear Truth

People have eyes and ears but they can see and hear only what exists inside their minds.

For example, you would not be able to read or understand English if you did not know English - if you did not "have" English within your mind. In the same way, a person who does not have Truth within him will not be able to understand when he is told of Truth.

No matter how much people are told of Truth, they cannot see or hear because they do not have Truth within them.

Let's Go, Let's Hurry

Let's go, let's go,

let's hurry to the world of nirvana;

let's go, let's go,

let's hurry to the eternal heaven we have only heard of;

let's go, let's go,

let's hurry to the world of Buddha;

let's go, let's go,

let's hurry to the world where divine beings live;

let's go, let's go,

let's hurry to the land of Truth.

Let's go to eternal heaven while we are living,

and while living, let's become immortals.

To be well-born: to be born as Truth

To live well: to live as Truth

To be good-looking: to have been born as Truth

Man believes the shadow is real;

holding onto it, he lives within it.

The Affairs Of The World Are All The Same

The affairs of the world are all the same.
When they pass, they are all dreams.
In a meaningless world,
people suffer loaded down with burdens,
and they are not able to laugh or cry -
a person with a dead consciousness blames the world,
and lives without knowing the true meaning or purpose.
Now that my long-sought dreams have been fulfilled,
and I have climbed over the *Arirang* hills,
now that I have become the master of all creations
and I have seen and become that
which I had previously only dreamt of - a divine being -
I now know that all affairs of human life
are meaningless.
Now I understand the crickets' chirping,
I understand the cicadas' song,
and I can properly see all living things.
Now that I have come to my true senses,
my heart is filled with joy.
When all people come to their senses,
when they escape from their suffering
and live properly,
the frustrations of my heart will be appeased.

One's Own Fault

The blue sky, green mountains and clear water
open wide the human mind.
People live their lives in the world
but they do not know where they come from,
why they live and where they will eventually go.
While in ignorance of the true meaning and purpose,
they blame the world and others
because nothing in the world suits their minds.
For them, all things are dissatisfactory,
and this remains in their minds.
They live foolishly with these regrets.
When will they go to the land where the world is alive?
People who are already there worry about those who are not.
Those who have not reached this world
are trapped inside themselves, speaking the words of ghosts,
and the people of the world are unable to distinguish whose words
    are true,
but moreover, they are not even interested.
They do not know that this is a matter of the utmost importance,
of life and death,
and they are simply unable to see or hear.
Ironically, the angry people are those who are in the wrong,

and they do not realize their wrong-doings at all.

No one knows what human life is,

no one knows where they are headed,

and indeed there is nowhere to go.

Everyone is insane -

they only say insane and crazy things.

The insane are running amok, not realizing they have gone crazy.

They believe their insanity is normal, that it is right.

Everything in the world is one's own fault,

and one must repent himself.

Know that everything in the world is your fault,

and if you discard yourself that is at fault,

you can live in the world

without hindrances or conflict.

Dear People, Let's Drink The True Water Of Life

Let's go over the *Arirang* hills,

Arirang, arirang, arariyo,

Passing over the *Arirang* hills.

He who forsakes me and leaves,

will go lame before he has gone a league.

- *Arirang*, a Korean folk song

Passing over the *Arirang* hills symbolizes both parting with one's self and gaining one's self.

Where it says that a person who leaves *me* will become lame means that a person who leaves his true self will become sick and die before getting too far. It signifies death. When one has passed over all the *Arirang* hills, he can drink the water of life.

By meeting one's true self, his false self will disappear. When this happens, no matter how hard he tries to recall having had a body in the past, he will just exist in the state where even the concept of the past has vanished. Passing over the *Arirang* hills also represents finding his complete true self.

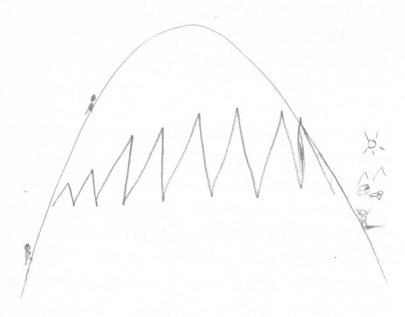

아제랑 고개 넘어 살자

Let's live beyond the *Arirang* hills.

What Happens When One Completely Becomes Truth

One is Truth only when he has become Truth completely.

Falseness is that which is not Truth.

Truth that has falseness in it, is not Truth.

Truth is only Truth when it is completely Truth.

If falseness and Truth are mixed together, it is not Truth.

A person is complete and Truth

only when he has become a hundred percent Truth.

This means he must know that his past self no longer exists,

and that he simply just exists.

This only happens when he is enlightened that he is perfect,

when his past self no longer exists at all, and only Truth remains.

Existence and non-existence become one

when the entire body of a person who has received the seal of Truth

on his forehead becomes the Soul and Spirit of Truth completely.

If he then becomes the mind of God,

he will become enlightened that he is complete.

This is what it is to drink from the fountain of life,

and this is a hundred percent Truth.

When death no longer exists for him,

he becomes an eternal and never-dying immortal,

and he becomes one hundred percent Truth.

Such a person does not have any curiosities,

he does not know anything, and he just lives,

without even the desire to know.

He can clearly see that people are dead

and only the mind that wants to save them remains.

He knows that he lives as an immortal in the everlasting world

and he lives as the Energy and Light of the Universe itself.

The Age Of Discrimination

There are no clouds in the pristine clear blue-black sky,

and even here on the earth in America, great nature is silent

and does not discriminate between you and me.

People however, discriminate between black, white and yellow.

Everyone's minds are different;

their minds are formed by the lives they lived,

and there is a lack of mutual understanding.

Now and in the past, people do not know man's nobility,

and although it cannot be seen

there is discrimination based on outward appearances.

The present world is one where people live with mutual wariness.

Enlightenment Is Faith

When we talk about faith, no one knows what faith is or how exactly one should believe.

Is it faith to read religious scriptures? Is it to donate a lot of money, or is it praying and singing hymns at the religious organization? Or is it perhaps to diligently attend morning prayers, or to go and pray in the mountains? No one knows what the standard for faith is.

Each religion seeks Truth, praises the existence of Truth, speaks of and listens to words of Truth. However, doing these things cannot make Truth theirs. In order for Truth to really become one's own, he must become enlightened. Enlightenment is what one comes to know when his consciousness grows bigger on his journey towards the infinite Energy and Light of the Universe which is the existence of Truth.

Consciousness is the mind, so therefore, when one's mind becomes this existence itself he can at last say that he has faith.

The way we live and what we say reflect what is in our minds.

A person who has Truth within him will live a life of Truth. For such a person, all the things he did not know about Truth will disappear. When one's mind completely believes, or in other words, when he has been completely enlightened, he will truly, truly, have faith.

Even A Saint Does Not Know His Flaws

An old Korean proverb tells us that even a saint does not know his own flaws. No one in the world knows he himself is a sinner and the worst person; all people believe that what they do is right and that they have done well.

Only people in levels seven and eight of the meditation who have cleansed a lot of their minds finally realize that they themselves are the worst people in the world. Perhaps one can only realize the faults or flaws of one's own mind in the level of human completion - beyond the state of sainthood.

The Only Sin Is Not Becoming One With Truth

There are many conceptions of sin in the world that strive to restrict our behavior. The Ten Commandments is one among many different lists of sins.

From the viewpoint of Truth, the only sin in the world is not becoming Truth and living as Truth. Nothing else is a sin. This is because one dies if he lives as a sinner with delusional falseness but he lives if he becomes Truth. It is possible to know that not becoming one with Truth is the only sin when one has become Truth.

Truth Does Not Disappear
No Matter How Much One Tries To Destroy It

The existence of Truth is the emptiness which existed before the emptiness of the infinite Universe.

This existence does not ever disappear, not in an eternal fire or when bashed by an iron plate that is infinitely wide. The existence of Truth always just exists. An existence that does not ever disappear no matter how one tries to destroy it - the existence that is always eternal and never-changing - is Truth. It is without a beginning or end, and it is an existence that exists of and by itself.

Religions, Philosophies, Ideologies And Books Tell Us As
Much As The Founder, Philosopher, Thinker, Or Author
Has Inside Them

When we know the origin, it is easy to understand all religions, philosophical ideas, ideologies, all schools of thought and books, and it is also easy to be able to tell when something has been said or written correctly or incorrectly. When we know the origin it is also possible to know everything that came from the human mind during the time of incompletion is false. Knowing the origin, which is Truth, allows us to master everything. Only this is Truth.

When we know the origin, we can know what is right and wrong in the world, without having read many books in the past or reading more books in the future.

There have always been cults and false religions. Jesus Christ was crucified because the Jewish people regarded him as being the leader of a cult and a false religion. In the early days of Christianity in Rome, people of the Christian faith were heavily persecuted. There are also similar cases in Korea - a Buddhist monk of the *Shilla* dynasty, *Ichadon*, died while spreading Buddhism and when Catholicism first entered the country, a Catholic priest, *Kim Dae Gun*, died while spreading Catholicism.

These kinds of things happened because the existing religions of the time which dominated over the area had fixed standards and beliefs about their religions. Anything that did not fit in with these standards and beliefs were condemned as being cults and false religions.

Two thousand years ago, people did not believe Jesus Christ when he said he was the Son of God. Due to the fact that he was Jewish and he also looked Jewish, he did not fit in their fantastical conceptions of what the Son of God should look like, and they told him that he could not be the Son of God because he was the son of a carpenter. Just as people did not recognize Jesus Christ, the Son of God, when Truth comes to the world no one will recognize him as being Truth.

The sort of Truth that fits one's conceptions and habits will never come, no matter how long he waits. God who is Truth dwelled inside Jesus Christ, but no one was able to see this. People thought he was not the Son of God based on his outer appearance.

When we walk down the street, it is not possible to know the professions of the countless people passing by, nor is it possible to know their inner levels of consciousness. In the same way, even when a person spreads and teaches Truth, those who are bound within their existing framework of minds will not be able to know or recognize the person who has Truth in him.

Even the Bible tells us that people look at the outer shape and form while Jehovah looks at the inner heart. People judge others however they please based on outer appearances, so a person whose mind is false and has false religions in it will judge others to be cults or false religions even when they are not. A person with a bigger mind than this will not do so.

People think only what is theirs is right, and other people are wrong. The fact is only one's self and what is one's own is wrong, but people do not know this because they lack wisdom.

From the viewpoint of Truth, anything that is not Truth is a cult. A false religion is something that speaks of Truth and is similar to Truth, but is not Truth and where one cannot become Truth. Anything that falls into the above category is a cult and a false religion.

Cults and false religions use the concept of "faith" to tie people down to their set framework of rules and beliefs but this is not right.

Truth is something that is large and all-encompassing - and therefore, people will follow it even if they are not told to do so. Is it faith to often go to the temple, mosque or church? Or is it faith to sing hymns and religious songs, attend morning prayers and read the religious scriptures? What decides what faith is? The definition of faith is to become Truth when one meets someone who is Truth. In order to become Truth, one must discard his self that he believes to be right. He must first escape from his conceptions and habits of what cults and false religions are, and discard himself that is a sinner. When one does this, only the existence of Truth remains and this existence becomes his self. This is what true faith is.

For example, simply saying that you like someone does not mean that you truly like him. In the same way, faith does not exist in words; it is only true faith when one's mind truly believes and when one's mind acknowledges and accepts.

One comes to have faith when he receives enlightenment, and enlightenment is what one comes to know as his mind changes to that of Truth.

Therefore, it can be said that enlightenment is faith. What the mind believes is enlightenment. The enlightenment of one's mind truly believing does not come from trying to take in "good" words.

Enlightenment comes only when one discards, and one receives as much enlightenment as he has discarded.

A person who has been completely enlightened is a person who has discarded everything, and a person who has been completely enlightened is a person who has completely achieved Truth.

Such a person is Truth so he truly believes in Truth. His actions are true and he lives a life of Truth because his mind is that of Truth.

From the first to the last level of Maum Meditation, the only thing that people do is to discard their selves that are sinners in order to become Truth itself. Anyone who claims that it is a cult or a false religion is a person who has never discarded himself and he is not a person of Truth. Because the consciousness or minds of people are becoming bigger and they are becoming Truth, he may feel that this threatens the sustainability of his organization.

If a person, organization or religion was righteous, it would allow people to try different things and guide them to the right path. Anyone who claims that only that which is theirs is right and all others are cults and false religions is himself of a false religion and a cult. Someone with a big mind accepts all things and does not claim only one thing is right.

Maum Meditation does not claim that only Maum Meditation is right. Not only does it not block its members from attending other organizations or religions; they do so freely. It is liberal. I think that there will be progress if religions that are restrictive became more liberal and they guided people toward the right path.

There is a Korean proverb which says that people like to throw ashes on a bowl of rice when they cannot eat it themselves. This means people like spoiling things for other people when they cannot take advantage of it. I write this in the hopes that in the world there are people with a conscience who will guide others to a place that can teach them properly if they cannot teach them themselves.

Will You Only Speak Of Truth
Or Will You Become Truth?

The age of incompletion was a time of only speaking of Truth. The age of completion is a time when anyone can achieve Truth, that is, one can become Truth.

When one only listens to words of Truth, he comes to have a delusional Truth of his conceptions and habits in his mind. A person who has become Truth is without death because he is Truth itself. He lives in the world that is without death, and he works for that world because he has wisdom.

A person who has become Truth is a person who has transformed into the Light and Energy of the Universe and he lives in this world. However a person who just listens to words of Truth is not Truth but a delusional hallucination and as such, is the personification of death.

The Human Mind

Everything in creation has the mind of its shape and form. The shape and form itself is its mind.

A person's mind is similar to the minds of his parents. His very form is given to him by his parents, and he resembles his parents in appearance and therefore, his mind also resembles theirs. He is born with the mind of his form, and he acquires further minds of attachment and self-centeredness through the life he lives. The human mind is the sum of these things.

Man's mind consists of the mind that he was born with, given to him by his parents, the minds he learned from his parents, as well as the minds he learned from his childhood, schools, other educational institutions, society and marriage. The minds he acquires through his experiences collectively forms a "self", a strong mind of attachment. Man believes that this is him. The shadows of past illusionary memories become him, and he lives out his life holding onto them.

It is because man has this mind that people's opinions, values, standards and judgments differ. Within the self-centered framework of "self" that is the human mind, man has put in his ideas of right and wrong. He lives according to this mind. There is a Korean saying that one lives according to the minds that he has "eaten".

This means that the way that one lives is no more and no less than the minds that he has within him.

For example, a person who studies medicine at school puts medicine into his mind. Therefore, he will earn his living from doing something in the medical field. A person who studies law will earn his living from the law and a person who studies computing will earn his living from the technology industry. How one behaves and how one lives is determined by what he holds in his mind, so one's life goes according to what minds he put inside himself. He lives in exactly that way, and to that extent only.

Therefore, it is when one discards his false delusional shadows of past memories - his own self - and he acquires the mind of Truth that he is able to truly live.

The human mind can be organized in the following way: It consists of two parts - one's remembered thoughts of the life that he has lived, and the mind of these thoughts which is the body itself. This mind is one that should be discarded for man is an entity that speaks and behaves according to what this illusionary mind orders him to do. Man believes that he is this mind.

However, he is merely living having become this framework of "self" formed from false delusions of past memories. Man suffers and is burdened because he can only speak, behave and live according to what he has in his mind. Becoming the Energy and Light of the Universe itself is to escape from this, and when he becomes Truth itself he becomes complete.

Man's body and mind are separate from each other, while a true person's body and mind are united - they are one. Such a person is complete Truth itself.

Such an existence is the living Energy and Light itself.

The Creator

The Creator is an existence that gives birth to all things in creation and it is also the master of all creations. This existence is the great living Soul and Spirit of the Universe that is omnipotent and omniscient.

Omnipotence is the role of the Soul and omniscience is the role of the Spirit. This existence existed an eternity before, and it will exist an eternity after. It is an existence that is living, and one that just simply exists, of and by itself.

This existence is without death. It is the mother and father of all creation as well as their master. All creations are its representations and they are this entity in the form of existence. It is said to be omnipotent because it creates all things, and it is omniscient because it knows that everything is one and alive.

People have called this existence *dō* (Truth or the Way) and they have also called it God, Buddha, *Haneol-nim*, Allah, the original nature, the original mind, the origin, the true mind and Truth. It has also been called the Creator, the divine light, *Jung-Shin*, *Sambhogakaya* and *Dharmakaya*, Soul and Spirit, Holy Spirit and Holy Father, the body and mind of the Universe, and emptiness and existence.

This existence is the Universe before the great Universe. The absolute emptiness of this existence is the Soul and the existence that exists amidst the emptiness is the Spirit. All creations in the Universe are one with this Soul and Spirit, and all things are alive except man who is trapped and dead within his delusions. Because this existence is living, every living thing in the Universe lives according to the will of *Jung* and *Shin*.

Man must return to this existence in order to become complete, and only then does eternal life and heaven exist for him. All creations are one with the Creator but at the same time, they are its children. They are one itself and alive, therefore the world is already enlightened and the world of God is already saved. However man is not one with this existence so not only does he live with suffering and burden, he is dead.

Man lives with the energy from the food he eats, but a true life only comes from when one transforms to the Energy and Light of the Creator. Without this, eternal life does not exist and neither does heaven. Just as the world is alive, man's mind must also become one with Truth. He must live with that mind of Truth for only then can he live forever. The existence of the Creator is Truth and therefore without death; an eternal and indestructible existence. Without being resurrected as the child of this existence, no one can live. The ultimate purpose of all religions is eternal life and heaven which can be achieved if man completely offers up his self and becomes one with this existence.

The land of this existence is without death and it is a place where only this existence lives. When man repents and is resurrected, it is the completion of all religions. It is then also the age of man becoming the master. It was the original Creator who created all things, and thus it is also the responsibility and the lot of the Creator to save all of creation. Only by the grace of the Creator can all creations and people live.

The Mind

The forms of all things are mind, and all things live according to their forms. Although mankind has studied the mind and what the mind is for a long time, no one has been able to define what it is, give its true meaning, or determine which minds we must discard. The Bible tells us that the poor in spirit (in this case, another term for "mind") are blessed, for the kingdom of heaven is theirs. We have also often heard that we must empty and cleanse our minds. However, we were not able to know exactly which minds we should empty and cleanse. No one knew what the mind's entity or form is, or in other words, what the mind is.

The original mind is the Energy and Light of Truth, the Universe before the infinite Universe. This existence existed an eternity ago, and it will exist an eternity later. It is the very essence of an eternal and never-dying immortal. All creations in the world are the representations of this existence. All creations in the world are this existence. The origin of the things in the world is this great Soul and Spirit of the Universe, which is the Creator, the sky before the sky and the Universe before the Universe. It is the mother and father of all things, it is our origin, and it is our original mind.

This existence is always alive, and it is Energy and Light that is Truth itself. Thus, it is without death and it is an existence that is omnipotent and omniscient. The reason we seek our original mind is in order to live forever in the heaven that never dies. This existence lives forever and always just exists, even if all things in the world disappear. It is Energy and Light itself, the source and origin of the great Universe. A person who has been reborn as this Energy and Light of the great Universe can live.

While people are alive, they sustain their lives from the energy of the food they eat but a person who has been born as the Soul and Spirit of the great Universe, as Energy and Light itself, while he is living does not die even after his body dies. If people cleanse their minds and are reborn as this true mind, death no longer exists for them.

People's minds are all different; they differ according to their shape and form. People's forms resemble their parent's forms; hence all people's minds are different from birth.

People are sinners because they are not one with Truth. It is said that man has original sin because he is born from his parent's sin, his parent's karma. People have bodies and minds; man's mind is an entity of original sin. By storing self-centered minds, false illusions that are shadows of the memories of the life he has lived, these minds have become him. He lives according to what these delusions of attachments order him to do, believing that they are him.

Man lives in a way that is no more and no less than these minds that he has put inside himself. If one has stored medical knowledge inside himself, he makes a living with this knowledge, and if he has stored the law inside himself, he makes a living from the law. While he lives, he continually stores more and more without discarding anything so he becomes a slave to these numerous minds and he lives with suffering, burdens and delusions.

Man's mind is not one; he has many, many different kinds of minds. Each of them orders him to do different things, which is why man is so fickle and his mind changes so frequently. If he is to discard these minds and find the true mind, he must throw away his illusionary life that he has within him, as well as his illusionary body that contains these illusionary minds. If he discards even the illusionary Universe in him, only the true mind remains.

The true mind is Truth. It is the great Soul and Spirit and it is the body and mind of Truth. He must be reborn as this Soul and Spirit in order to never die and live in the right way. This place, here, must become heaven if he is to live in heaven after he dies. The mind that one must discard is his mind of attachments, his mind of false images. He must also eliminate his body that contains his mind and the Universe that is in the illusion. Then only the mind of Truth remains and he can be reborn as this mind. This is what Maum Meditation is. Maum Meditation is not about blaming others; it is about killing and discarding one's own self who is at fault. From beginning to end, it is about discarding one's self and being reborn as the existence of Truth, the true mind, when one no longer exists.

The True Meaning Of Salvation

The number of new religions in Korea rose considerably during a certain period of time, and around the world there are innumerable new religions. The ultimate message of all religions is that one day the existence of Truth will come to save the world. Buddhism told us that *Maitreya* will come to the world and Christianity told us that Jesus, the Savior, will come again. Other religions have also said that such an existence will come to the world. While the names used for this existence in each religion is different, the fundamental meaning behind them is that a complete existence of Truth will come and enable all people to become Truth.

New religions form when someone claims to be the Savior. Even now, many people believe and follow such people. The true meaning behind a religion is to follow the teachings of Truth. It is also to follow and believe that Truth will come to the world. The constant conflicts between religions will only come to an end when the existence of Truth finally does come.

People do not know what is true and false, because they have no wisdom. They are trapped inside their delusions and because they are unable to tell what is truly true and false, they judge whether something is right or wrong based on their experiences. If something fits their fixed conceptions, they believe it to be right and they believe everything else to be wrong. It is impossible for people to know what Truth actually is, because they live bound to their conceptions and habits.

People do not know Truth because their entire worlds are lived inside falseness, without being able to see, understand or become Truth.

Salvation is making people able to become Truth. If someone has become Truth, he has been saved. He is saved when his delusional soul is reborn as the Soul of Truth; when his delusional soul is reborn as the body and mind of the Universe's origin: *Jung* and *Shin*, *Sambhogakaya* and *Dharmakaya*, the Holy Ghost and Holy Father, or Energy and Light itself. Without becoming the existence of Truth himself, eternal life and heaven cannot exist for him; it is death.

Salvation is to live; salvation is to become Truth; and salvation is to be reborn as the never-changing Energy and Light. It is living forever in the land of Energy and Light that is Truth.

The True Mind

The Soul and Spirit of the great Universe is Truth, and this is the true mind.

A person who has been resurrected as this true Soul and Spirit has a true mind. If he has been reborn with the true mind while he is living, he is Truth itself and therefore he can truly live. The true mind is the mind of Truth. He is the Soul and Spirit of Truth so he is free from death.

The true mind is the mind that contains absolutely nothing. The true mind is the mind of Truth and it is a mind that just exists without a past or a future. It is the mind that is without discrimination and discernment, and it is a mind where everything has ceased.

It is a mind that knows nothing, and is without curiosity, doubts and suspicions. It is a mind that is without "self". It does not even contain the thought that it exists so it is Truth itself, and therefore it has the wisdom of knowing Truth. It is a mind that knows that all people at present are insane, and it knows that all people are dead. It knows that all people speak only from their own viewpoints and it is a mind that knows that people do not actually know anything.

The true mind is the Energy and Light itself of the Universe. This mind knows eternal life that is without death with the wisdom that comes from this existence. It is without death because it is eternal life itself. It knows Truth because it is Truth, and it lives in the land of Truth forever.

Where Heaven Is And How To Get There

The ultimate purpose and desire of all religions is to go to heaven and live there.

Heaven is a place where people live forever. A place that lives eternally is the land of Truth. That land is the Universe before the Universe and the sky before the sky. It is a spiritual land, a land of *Jung* and *Shin*. It is the land where only those who have become the Energy and Light of the Universe which is *Jung* and *Shin* itself live. A person who has been reborn as the body and mind of this existence is one who has gone to this land.

Such a person is one who has become Truth itself and whose individual self has been resurrected as Truth; a person who has become Truth and both the individual and the whole have been born in the land of Energy and Light. Then heaven exists. It is a land where one's self no longer exists, and only the Energy and Light of the great Universe remains, and he who has been born as this Energy and Light live there. It can be found inside a person who has *Jung* and *Shin* within him, a person who has become the heart of the great Universe. It exists within one's mind and the way to get there is to be without "self" and be reborn as the *Jung* and *Shin* of the Universe.

Life And Death (Heaven And Hell)

The ultimate purpose of all religions is to live forever and live in heaven. When we have bodies we live with the energy from the food we eat, but after our bodies pass away those who have the eternal and never-changing Truth within them will live because they are Truth and those who have delusions within them will die because their very selves are illusions. Namely, those who have delusions will die because they live in a false delusional world.

The true principle of the Creator who created the world is for existence to give birth to existence and save them in the land of Truth forever.

All of the many things in creation are already enlightened. This means that they are one with Truth and thus, they are alive. However, people are dead because of their selfish minds and attachments - they are dead because their consciousnesses are not one with Truth.

Life and death are actually one. This is because a person, whose consciousness has been enlightened of Truth that is the Creator, is himself Truth, and he lives because Truth is alive. However, a person whose delusions have become him is like a dream, an illusion - it is the illusion that lives, but an illusion is not truly alive or real so it is dead.

When we talk about going to heaven or hell, what heaven and hell truly mean is that a person who has returned to the infinite Creator of the Universe, to Truth itself, and has been reborn will live in heaven while a person who lives in delusions will be in hell.

Heaven is this world just as it is, but people do not have heaven inside their minds. Therefore, they are unable to see or know it.

Man speaks and lives exactly according to what he holds in his mind. His mind only contains what he has experienced, and he believes that these things are him. If he discards the body and mind of the false delusional entity that he calls himself and even the Universe, true Truth remains. It is only when Truth remains, and he becomes Truth, that he can know Truth.

Man must escape from his self, the delusional entity of attachments, and be reborn as the existence of Truth. Only then does heaven and eternal life exist for him.

There is a Korean saying, that one can know the afterworld only after he has died. This means that when one does not exist and he has returned to the Creator, he can know not only the principles of the world but also the oneness of life and death. Because man only knows what he has experienced, it is only when he has Truth inside him, that is, when he has become the viewpoint of the infinite Creator of the Universe, that he can know everything. And it is then that he can live because he is Truth.

Eternal life is to live as the Soul and Spirit, the existence of Truth. In other words, if one is born as the Energy and Light of the Universe itself, he is without death and he lives in the land of that Energy and Light. Such is what heaven is. When man's consciousness transforms into the consciousness of Truth, he lives a true life because his consciousness is alive.

Even if his body disappears, his Soul and Spirit lives here in this land, the living land of Truth, forever. Anything that has not become the Energy and Light of the Universe is dead and lives in hell.

Heaven is not a place that one goes to after death. A person who goes to heaven while he is living is a person who lives forever.

The reason Maum Meditation is causing a sensation around the world is because it has the scientific meditation method that allows one to eliminate his body and mind - his false mind - and go to the everlasting world while he is living by becoming reborn as Truth.

Cults And That Which Are Real And Fake

A few years ago, I visited Mexico. Mexico is a high altitude country with a high crime rate. Mexico City is located in one of the valleys of the mountain ranges, sitting atop a lake so despite its high altitude, it is one of the cities with the worst air pollution in the world. When you first arrive, it can be dizzying and the amount of pollution can make your face sting.

The majority of the Korean people who live in South America own and run small stores; clothing stores, gift stores, household product stores and so on. In the past, most fruit stalls and laundry stores in the U.S. were run by Jewish people but were eventually taken over by Koreans who thought that there was good money to be made. Similarly, Koreans have taken over most of the clothing stores that were originally operated by Jewish people.

Many Koreans who were living in Argentina came to Mexico. They sold knock-off clothing with the real label stuck on, but later suffered for it when they were reported to the authorities by Jewish people. Apart from clothes, there are many fake things in the world posing as the real thing.

Particularly in religion, philosophy and ideology - areas that are related to spiritual matters - no one knows how to tell the difference between what is real and fake.

Commonly, anything that is not one's own is condemned as being a cult and a false religion. But in any case, anything that is not real must be a fake.

In that case, what is real?

Truth is what is real, and anything that is not Truth is fake, even if one tries to become Truth and listens to words of Truth.

It is possible for anyone to know that they have not become complete. Therefore, when one discards his false self, his true self will remain. However, people find it difficult to become real because they try to do so while retaining their false selves.

A false religion is something that is similar to the real thing. However, if you cannot become real through it, it is false. All people say that their religion is the true one, but it is not if they themselves have not become real, even if they speak words of Truth and try to behave like Truth.

One must have become complete Truth in order to say that he is real. Most people do not realize that they are being fooled in some way.

That which is real can tell both what is real and false, but that which is false does not know either. One must become real to realize that he himself is false and that he himself is wrong. If he himself has not become real, then everything is false and a false religion.

In that case, all places apart from the place where one can discard his false self and become real may be false. Man does not have wisdom so he has a tendency to claim that what is his is right even though he has not become real and complete. When someone claims that something or somebody else is a cult or a false religion, it is because he himself is so.

A person who claims such things has false religions and cults inside his mind. If they did not exist in his mind, he would not do so.

If one discards himself and achieves human completion, he becomes real and the place that guided him is also real. The places where one cannot become real are all false; they are the cults and false religions.

In the many ages that have been, that person of that time.

Part 4

A Talk With Joe Gattis, An American Priest Who Has Achieved Completion

Joe Gattis : Can one really become Truth? Can anyone really become Truth?

Woo Myung : Anyone can become Truth. By repenting one's sins, when the existence that is one's self, and the delusional Universe that one's delusions created is gone, only Truth remains.

A Talk With Joe Gattis, An American Priest Who Has Achieved Completion

Woo Myung What changes did you experience in yourself after you did the meditation?

Joe Gattis Let me tell you about my Maum Meditation experience. I suffered from depression my whole life. I also suffered from intense back pain and migraines and I could only sleep 4-5 hours a night. And a few years before I began Maum Meditation, I developed asthma.

In the year that I started the meditation, my closest friend passed away and I was in a near suicidal state. On 30th December in 2002, I was driving home from work and I decided that I would kill myself when I got home by taking some pills. But when I got home, I forgot, and I only remembered when I got up the next morning.

That day at work, a Korean colleague at work told me about Maum Meditation so I made an appointment to visit the meditation center in Atlanta. Not only did I want to go and find out what Maum Meditation was about, I was told that I would be given a free meal, and I was not about to pass that up!

I went at lunchtime and I talked with several people about spiritual matters, the Universe, and the false self. In the seminar that followed, I learned about the true mind versus the false mind, and about the infinite Universe.

By truly repenting, my life completely changed for the better. Around the end of the first meditation session, I could feel my hands begin to tremble. And that night, for the first time in a long time I slept deeply for ten whole hours and woke up, pain-free. Miraculously, my ashen face was tinged with pink and my depression, asthma and migraines disappeared. I felt that this meditation was too great to keep to myself, and I wanted to learn it and teach it to others so that they too could reap its benefits.

After that, I completed all the levels and became a meditation instructor.

Thank you for bringing Truth to the world so that we can become free from our delusional worlds and become Truth.

Woo Myung Where do you think you would be if you had not done this meditation?

Joe Gattis I would have died. Even if I hadn't killed myself, I would have spent my life dead inside my false mind, and unable to see the world as it is because of my conceptions.

Woo Myung Joe, what did you think of me when you first met me?

Joe Gattis When I first saw you, I felt a peace that I had not felt from anyone before. And you asked me if I thought that you were Truth.

I wondered who you were, that you would ask me such a question. I answered, and you laughed. Then we spent many hours talking just as we are doing now.

The next week, you asked me the same question and I answered then that I didn't know. Again, you laughed and we spent another week talking.

You asked me again a third time if I thought that you were Truth and that time, I answered yes. You did not laugh but instead began to teach me about the mind in earnest.

Woo Myung What difference has Maum Meditation made in your life?

Joe Gattis Before doing Maum Meditation, my life was full of darkness, pain and suffering from which I was unable to escape. Because I was evil and sinful, I would first make those around me like me and then treat them badly. But I was under the delusion that I was living my life as best as I could. I thought that I lived for others, but in fact I lived only for myself.

After Maum Meditation, I no longer suffer from mental and physical pain as I did before. Now that I have the Universe, I do not feel that I lack anything and I no longer worry. I feel that I can finally truly help others and now I only think about how I can save people. I no longer only think of myself. This is because if there is no "me", then there is no "me" to feel suffering either.

The world is clearer, brighter and filled with peace and happiness. When meditation students talk to me about their woes and worries, what they say passes through me and it does not give me pain or suffering. At the same time, I can understand their suffering because I have also gone through what they are experiencing: the life inside a tomb. It makes me want to help them even more, so that they can be resurrected as Truth and live in heaven.

I have gained everything because I discarded everything. So I want to thank you again.

Woo Myung How has your life improved after doing the meditation?

Joe Gattis The first thing that changed was my health. Apart from what I told you earlier, I lost 60 pounds, and the scoliosis (curvature of the spine) miraculously straightened itself. My eye-sight got better, and my stamina increased. I also found that I stopped becoming attached to events that happened around me. But these external changes are trivial compared to the changes within. Now, I have a meaning and purpose for living. I want to work to save others selflessly. The continuous thoughts that ran through my head have stopped and my mind that has been emptied is able to see the Universe. I can see nature's flow and I am growing wiser. I no longer see things through my delusions, instead I see them just as they are.

I used to be attached to the forms, shapes and colors of things but I no longer see the Universe with my false mind.

Now I live in heaven, here, with the true mind.

Woo Myung Why do you think people should do Maum Meditation?

Joe Gattis These things are not possible without doing Maum Meditation. However, they are incidental to the real reason people must do Maum Meditation, which is that people must become one with Truth and return to the Universe. By doing so, they return to God and can live forever in heaven.

In the last year, many students have asked me questions about Maum Meditation. And I would like to ask you those questions. What is it like to live in heaven?

Woo Myung Heaven is the land where Truth lives. Therefore, it is the land where those whose minds are one with God, the Creator of the great Universe live; those who do not have individual minds live, in fact the individual does not exist; and where those who have been born again as the great Universe's God himself live. It is a land where only Truth lives, so it is without worries, anxieties or suffering. It is the freedom of freedoms, and there are no conflicts or blockages because there is no self. There, one has no self although he exists. He exists but he does not have the mind that he exists. This mind does not exist, but the mind exists.

Because one is free from himself, it is liberation; because there is no self it is freedom. Heaven is living forever in the land of Truth without want.

Such a mind has nothing in it other than the mind of one, and this mind is the Creator itself. Therefore, one lives forever. In the land of the Energy and Light which created all things, one lives as an individual.

One lives according to nature's flow, as the mind of nature does. In that mind, there is boundless joy, and it is without anger, enemies, sadness, death, birth, sickness and aging. It is the land where one just lives, without these minds.

Only he who has been born as Truth in the land of Truth while he is living can go there.

Only those who have become one, Truth, can live together forever in that heaven. Doesn't it sound fantastic?

Joe Gattis Please explain to me about Adam and Eve's original sin.

Woo Myung If you look in the Bible, it tells us that there were people - the origin of mankind - before Adam and Eve.

Theologians hypothesize that the Garden of Eden was located near the rivers Euphrates and Tigris. It seems mankind, one race, lived nomadically, moving from one place to another according to the conditions of their environment and settled in the Garden of Eden where there were good conditions for life.

Adam and Eve were sinners, so people, all mankind, are also sinners because we are the children of sinners. When a demon - a sinner - has a child, the child is the offspring of a demon; hence, we are the offspring of demons. That is why we have original sin. When it is said that a serpent tempted Adam and Eve to eat the fruit of good and evil, it means that they had the cunning minds of vipers. As agricultural settlers, they began to decide what was sin and not sin by making rules. When someone broke the rules, they began to think they committed a sin and stored these thoughts in their minds. The storing of these thoughts is expressed as "eating". The mind of "goodness" is storing inside one's mind the good things that he has done. Storing one's subjective conceptions of good and evil is what "eating" the fruit of good and evil is.

This mind is not one with God; it is a self-centered mind of an individual's attachments, so therefore this mind itself is sin. A sinful mind and a sinful body are one so when we were born from the bodies of our sinful ancestors in a long line of sinful ancestors, we were born with original sin. We are all original sinners.

As we live, we commit actual sin so repenting our original and actual sin and becoming one with God is the absolution of sin.

One can only be saved when he is free from sin.

Joe Gattis Does everything come to an end when one dies? Or is there life after death?

Woo Myung When God created the world and all things in it, they were created to be complete and therefore, already saved. The expressions "the world is already enlightened" and "the world is already saved" have the same meaning. Among all the people there have been in the world, and everyone living in the world now, no one has ever known this. Even if they did know, no one has spoken clearly about it. In other words, there was no method for salvation.

In the infinite Universe, there is a Soul and Spirit, the original Creator. In modern scientific terms, it is called Energy and Light.

When the Creator, the Energy and Light, created all things in the world, they were created as Energy and Light, Truth, themselves. However, people are sinners because only they have self-centered minds that care only about themselves. They are dead and need to be saved, because they are trapped within themselves and are unable to become one with the Energy and Light, the Creator.

In the same way that how people live reflect what they hold in their minds, they can truly live only when inside their minds, they transform into the Energy and Light which is Truth.

A person who has transformed into Truth will live forever in the eternal and indestructible land of Energy and Light because such a world is life itself. The life that one has lived that is past is not Truth; so therefore a person who has not transformed into Truth only has the false mind of this life. Therefore, he dies because this mind is not Truth.

Just as a dream is an illusion that does not exist although it may seem to exist, living inside an illusion is hell.

Heaven is the place where one who has become Truth lives, and hell is a non-existent illusionary world where one who has not become Truth lives.

Joe Gattis What happens after death for a person who has committed suicide?

Woo Myung   A person commits suicide because he is narrow-minded; because of his selfish and self-centered mind. While a humble person can live under any circumstances, many people commit suicide when things do not go their way or when they cannot accept something in the world because of their strong pride.

They are people who are full of false minds due to their greed. They all receive the suffering of hell that is an illusion, and just as dreams are false, such things are dreams and are dead.

Joe Gattis   Is it possible to discard the life that you have lived after physical death?

Woo Myung   When a person dies, he cannot discard because only the hallucinations of his falseness remain. Namely, he is truly dead. Even if he could discard, it is not possible to teach him because Truth does not exist in a world of hallucinations, or in other words, in a false world.

Joe Gattis   Many people ask if Maum Meditation is a religious organization.

Woo Myung   Religions up to this point in time were organizations that believed in a particular person and read and listened to his words. However in Maum Meditation we only discard and eliminate ourselves, in order to become the existence of Truth, the Creator. Only the Creator which is the absolute existence is Truth. As one discards and eliminates himself, only the existence of Truth remains and since this existence is one's self, he becomes complete.

Isn't there a Korean expression, that there is no one to believe in but yourself? A person who has discarded and eliminated all of his self, and is therefore self-less, is reborn as Truth and the Creator, so he therefore believes his own mind, his own self. Because he is complete, he does not need religion for he does not need to believe in anything; he is religion itself.

Although Maum Meditation is only a place where one discards and eliminates himself, many people wonder if it is a religious organization because many people come to practice here. However, one does not believe in anything here; by simply eliminating one's self, the sinner, the individual can become Truth and complete, and so therefore, Maum Meditation can be called a trans-religion - one that transcends religion.

Such a person is complete, and is beyond religion. He himself is religion itself - a complete person. He believes therefore, in himself.

Joe Gattis Is everything inside the Universe false minds?

Woo Myung Originally, the world is already complete. It is man that is not complete. He is dead inside a mind that is only as big as himself, so therefore man is false. None of the other creations in the Universe have a mind of "self" and therefore, they are all alive. From the perspective of Truth that is one, everything is alive - it is man that is the problem, for it is his individual self that is dead.

Everything in the Universe is all real; that is to say, it is all real for a person who has become real but for a person who is false, it is all false.

Joe Gattis Buddha taught compassion, and Jesus taught love. You teach nature's flow. What is nature's flow?

Woo Myung The original mind, the mind of Truth, is compassion and love. Nature's flow is the mind of nature: the Universe, Truth, gives us food to eat, water to drink, gives us heat and cold, and allows all things to live, but it never expects anything in return. It does not have the mind of having done something, despite all it does; the very thought of having done something does not exist. Such a mind is the mind of nature's flow.

Even though it saves people, not having the thought, the mind, that it has done so is the mind of nature and great love, namely, it is nature's flow.

The mind of nature's flow is the mind of nature, one that is without "self". Therefore, it is without conflict and hindrances, and though it exists, it is a big mind that is accepting of all things. The mind of God that accepts everything is what nature's flow is.

Joe Gattis The people who are in the process of meditating ask what kind of benefits Maum Meditation has for their family and friends.

Woo Myung When we are dreaming, we do not realize that we are in a dream but when we wake up from the dream, we realize that we were struggling inside a non-existent illusion. In the same way, people's lives are the same as a dream; we are living inside a dream. Life is falseness itself, but when one wakes up from one's life that is a dream and becomes real it is possible to know that the life one is living is an illusion and a dream.

Maum Meditation makes falseness become real. Heavy burdens and suffering, events of great pain, of physical sickness, enemies and loved ones, anger, joy, aging and death exist within the illusion, but when one becomes real these delusional hallucinations disappear. Death does not exist, and one lives born in heaven. This is the work of Maum Meditation.

Joe Gattis What is the body and mind of the Universe?

Woo Myung The sky of the huge Universe where there is absolutely nothing is the Creator; it is the body of the Universe that creates all things and it is also the origin of all creations. It is the *Soul*. In the midst of absolute emptiness, only the one God exists, and this is the mind of the Universe's Creator. This is also called *Spirit*. The Universe is this huge Soul and Spirit itself. This is the body and mind of the Universe, and in Buddhism it was named *Sambhogakaya* and *Dharmakaya*. In Christianity, it was called Holy Spirit and Holy Father. In Korea which is rooted in the *Haneol* philosophy, it was called *Jung* and *Shin*. It is also called Energy and Light. Man's body as well as the bodies of all creations came from the body of this Creator, and although each creation has its own form and shape, there exists the one God.

Joe Gattis How can we know when Jesus has returned?

Woo Myung *Jesus* means the existence of Truth, the Creator, but just as people cannot see the Soul and Spirit of the Universe, no one can recognize Jesus. That is why it was said that he will come as a thief in the night, and that no one will know. It is said that only

God would know. The reason man cannot know is because man only sees with his eyes, and therefore only sees the outward appearance of things. Just as no one knows the professions of those he passes in the street, or the consciousness that they have within, man cannot see or know the person who has the Soul and Spirit of the Universe, the Creator, within him. If one is to know when Jesus has returned, he must become Jesus himself.

Falseness cannot see or know the existence that is real, but that which is real knows both that which is real as well as that which is false. Therefore, one must be real in order to know. A person whose sins are relatively light will hear the words of Truth more easily, and so it will be easier for him to repent. We must focus on making people become real. In other words, when one becomes real he will be able to recognize the new Messiah.

Joe Gattis Must one discard both good and bad memories when he meditates?

Woo Myung What man believes to be good and bad all exists within his false mind. We are asked to discard both because good and bad exist inside the false mind.

Joe Gattis What is sin? Does it mean the same as karma?

Woo Myung There is only one sin in the world, and that is not being one with Truth. Man's self-centered individual mind of attachments is sin, and it is because of this sin that he is unable to become one with Truth. Since he is not Truth, he is falseness. This is sin and death.

Sin and karma are different in name, but they are the same. Karma is one's self, that he has acquired. This self is not able to become one with Truth that is God, so therefore it is falseness and sin.

Joe Gattis Where do people go after they die?

Woo Myung People live their lives exactly according to what they have in their minds, no more and no less. And in the same way, a person who has illusions inside his mind lives in an illusion, the world of hell, whereas a person who has Truth inside his mind is Truth and thus lives forever in the world of Truth, the world of the Universe's Energy and Light.

Joe Gattis Is there a quick way, a short-cut, to becoming Truth?

Woo Myung All people have many sins, so there are no short-cuts. However it can be said that a person who has relatively less sins is more easily able to accept. Such a person listens and does what he is asked. This can be called the short-cut. Along the path to the absolution of one's sins, everyone believes himself to be great and shows his true colors. He is expressing the form of his sins. Basically the demon that believes it is great is showing itself. A person who knows his wrongdoings will repent, while a person who is ignorant of his wrongdoings will not repent, and eventually die by his sins. If one does the first level (of the meditation) and felt that it was good, the shortcut is to do the next level with gratitude. If he found the second level to be good, then again doing the next level with a thankful heart, and then the next, and the next again, is the short-cut. A person who has thankfulness has the short-cut, and such a person can be absolved of all his sins.

Joe Gattis Where is God?

Woo Myung There is nowhere in the world that God does not exist, and God is an immortal existence that exists in all creations, of and by himself. God exists within one who has become this existence, and for such a person he has God. God exists everywhere within the infinite Universe, which is the mind of one who has become Truth.

Joe Gattis Can one really become Truth? Can anyone really become Truth?

Woo Myung Anyone can become Truth.

By repenting one's sins, when the existence that is one's self, and the delusional Universe that one's delusions created is gone, only Truth remains. This existence of Truth becomes one's self. Anyone who has the will to achieve can do so. The Bible tells us that the door will open for all who knock - the door will not open for those who do not knock, but it will open for all those who do.

Part 5

The Land Of Light

Though there may be clouds in the sky, the sky itself just exists. Regardless of whether countless celestial bodies exist the sky itself just exists. Whether or not people exist, and whether or not all creations exist, the sky itself just exists.

The Land Of Light

Dusk is approaching,
but people do not know where to go.
They do not have anywhere to rest
because they have nowhere to go.

Immature people -
they live in the harshness of their realities
and hold onto them.
Pass over the *Arirang* hills
before night falls;
shed your burdens and sufferings,
so that you can know where you must go,
and find a place to rest.

If where you are is unfit for life,
you will be fine if you leave.
Why do people live in a place unfit for life?
People do not know their countless struggles
do not exist when they leave them;
this is the reason they have nowhere to go or rest.

Try living in the world beyond the *Arirang* hills -

it is freedom and liberation there,

because one's self of attachments does not exist.

Even if you live only for a day,

you must live as a living person;

even if you live only for a day,

you must live as Truth.

Only then can you shed your sufferings and burdens.

Why do you not know this,

and simply cry?

You may speak of your greatness,

you may brag that you are great,

but it is all a futile dream during a moment's nap.

People live with all kinds of events in their hearts

they do not have to have, as if they were treasures,

events of heartbreak as well as countless others,

but aren't these things suffering and burden?

Let's leave, let's leave,

let's go over the *Arirang* hills

to the world beyond.

All people in the world,

let's all leave -

To where there is no death, or even one's past self;

let's drink the water of life and shed suffering and burden.

Let's leave to the world of enlightenment,

a world of freedom,

a world of one,

a world where I am the master -

let's live in the world I have made.

In a place of many words,

it may seem as though people care for others

but they are envious and they begrudge others' successes.

A place of many words

only brings suffering.

Beyond the hills,

there is the land of Light.

One's forehead, one's mind is shone with light,

in the land of Light.

One is given new clothes from head to toe - a new body and mind -

he receives a whole body of Light.

If one goes to the land of Light,

the life that he has lived in the past does not exist,

and if one goes to the land of Light,

and one no longer has a past or future,

and like Light, there is no beginning or end,

he just exists.
By drinking the water of life, of Light,
I have become the Light.
Oh wanderers with nowhere to go,
let's all go to the land of Light
and drink the water of life.
Those who drink will live,
and for those who do not, it is death.

When the master, the Light, asks us to come,
without any restrictions, to the land of Light,
let's just go, without dallying in preparation.
Let's just go and live.
When one goes over the *Arirang* hills,
and drinks the water of life,
he has no death, and no self with suffering.
He becomes an eternal and imperishable immortal.

Let's go, let's go, let's hurry,
let's go drink water in the land of Light.
The water is light,
and this body becomes Light -
one is reborn as Energy that is Light.

A Person Who Has The Mind Of One Lives Well

Only a person who is as steadfast as a bear
can go to the world of Truth.

An agile and nimble tiger who has many talents,
has more attachments to his reality,
and his reality is easier for him
than going to the world of Truth.

All creations in the world are alive,
everything in the world is alive,
but man is dead;
man cannot go to heaven.

For a person who has the sky within him,
the sky is right where he is, here,
and for a person who has the sky within him,
heaven exists within him.

Only those who have escaped from themselves can live -
those who have become the Energy and Light of the great
  Universe.
Therefore man cannot live

without becoming Truth.

He who has countless minds in his mind
cannot be like the constant bear,
for those delusional thoughts are what tigers are.

Only a person like a bear -
a person who just lives, and just does,
whose mind does not flit back and forth -
can go to heaven.

Only when everything in the world exists in man,
does heaven, earth and man become one.
Only when man is the master of all things in heaven and earth
does everything become one.

At this time, all things are the mind of one,
of one heart,
the empty mind of cessation;
yet one can know everything
and live a life without want,
because such a person has everything.

Only the Creator is alive,
and only a person who has become the Creator can live.

Tigers are dead,
and tigers live in the world of hell.

Let's become a bear,
let's become a bear.
Let's not use our shallow cunning minds,
the minds of our forms, our false selves,
let's not use the resourceful mind of a tiger.

A person who believes himself to be clever
causes his own downfall with his cunning.
The most blessed is he who just exists,
and it is such a person who is able to achieve Truth.

Even in the worldly world,
a person who thinks too much is unable to succeed,
but a bear-like person silently does what he has to do,
and is able to achieve his will.

The greatest person in the world
is he who is able to be with all people,
and live by another's will.
A person who simply does his work
from a place beyond success and failure,
is a person with a big mind,

and it is into such a mind that blessings can enter.
People are unable to receive blessings
because they believe themselves to be great.

People's downfall is their own cunning,
their own greatness is their downfall.
When a person lives with the mind of one,
where existence and non-existence
of the Universe are one,
everyone can live well,
and this world can become a good place to live.

The reason people are unable to live good lives
is not because they lack a certain mind -
it is because they have too many minds.
This is the reason they are unable to achieve anything.
Man lives and dies inside these minds,
and he lives on with these minds even after death.

Let's learn how to just live.

호랑이는 사람이 못되고
곰은 참아서 사람된다

A tiger cannot become a human being,
but a bear can because he can endure.

The Will Of Heaven (The Sky)

I used to wonder

if there was something up there,

far up high in the blue sky.

Now I know the principles of heaven,

there is absolutely nothing in the sky

but yet there is God and Body, which is life.

All creations in the world are the expressions of this existence

  itself.

However, people live holding onto the shadows of their lives,

so only a person who knows the will of heaven

knows the principle that everything in man

is meaningless and false.

Man's Sin

Due to man's conceptions and habits,

he is trapped inside the framework of his self,

and thus, he is not one with Truth.

This is man's sin.

Having a self is sin.

There is only one sin that man can commit -

it is not being one with Truth.

This is the only sin there is.

It is said that man was made to resemble God,

and this means man's mind was made

to become one with God.

When all human minds are eliminated,

and one is reborn as Soul and Spirit,

which is the mind of the Creator,

he resembles the Creator.

Resemblance here does not mean that the two are similar;

Resemblance here means that the two are the same,

and that he is this existence itself.

A person who resembles the Creator is a person of one,

a person who resembles the Creator is Truth.

He becomes God himself.

In order to resemble God,

he must eliminate his self completely,

even the Universe of his conceptions.

Then, only Truth, the origin, remains.

This is absolution of sin,

and this is the way to become Truth.

He who has many things in his conscious and subconscious mind,

cannot become one with Truth because of what he possesses.

When what he possesses is gone, he is oneness itself.

The True Meaning Of "It Does Not Exist Yet It Does, It Exists But It Does Not"

It is often said that the place of the mind
does not exist -
that the place of the mind is non-existence.
People say that it does not exist
because they see it from their own minds.
It is the same for non-existence.
With human eyes, and from the human mind,
the Creator of the Universe does not exist -
it is non-existence.
But when one has become the mind of God,
in other words, when he has become the Creator itself,
he is able to see God.
Only a person who has the mind of the Creator itself
is able to see God.
When one's self is gone and only God remains,
when he has become God,
he is able to see God.
It is expressed as,
"it does not exist yet it does,
it exists but it does not"
because man must be taught through words.

The whole Universe came forth and was created

because God is alive.

When man sees heaven, which is the place of the mind,

and when the Universe exists in the mind of man,

it does not exist; it is non-existence.

But when man dies, and only God remains,

he who has become God can know that God exists.

He who has become God is born in the land of God,

of Energy and Light,

and can live as an eternal immortal.

This existence is alive and exists,

but man cannot see this God because of the human mind.

Only when man who has eliminated all of himself and the
    Universe in his mind while he is living,

in other words, only a person who has completely died for God is
    able to see.

That it exists but does not, does not exist but exists

means all things exist, but do not exist,

do not exist, and yet they do.

It means these states are one.

It means God exists, so heaven, earth and man exists,

and heaven, earth and man themselves are God.

He Who Has Completely Died

Let's imagine for a moment,
that right now there is an earthquake.
Even if I die in the earthquake,
doesn't the Universe still exist, just as it is?
A person who has become this Universe itself
is a person who has been reborn and resurrected.
If within one's lifetime
one becomes the Universe itself and is reborn,
he becomes an eternal immortal who does not die
even when his body dies.
He who has completely died,
is a person whose mind is Truth.
A person who has completely died
is he who dies, along with all creations in the Universe,
with only Energy and Light, the source of the Universe, remaining.
When he is reborn as this existence itself, as Energy and Light,
he is sealed on the forehead with light,
and his entire body becomes light.
When one becomes the heart of Truth itself,
and he is enlightened that he is complete,
his past no longer exists,
and he is an everlasting and eternal immortal

who just exists, as he is.

The completion of man is to become reborn as God,

as Energy and Light itself, which is Truth.

Such a person has become complete.

A person who has died without anything remaining,

has absolutely no individual minds;

he knows absolutely nothing

and has no delusional thoughts whatsoever.

He is alive, but even existence does not exist for him,

and he is God who just lives.

He lives as long as the age of the Universe.

This land of light never dies,

it is a place that exists.

The Will Of God

The will of God is the mind of non-existence
where absolutely everything has ceased.
God is alive so his will is to save
heaven, earth, man, and all things.
The completion of God
is to make all things in existence become God
and save them eternally by making them become
Energy and Light in the land of God.
This is God's will.
The master of the land of God
is God, a person, in existence.
The life of existence exists because man exists
and if man does not exist,
none of it has any meaning.

A person who has become God is the master,
and according to the will of the person who has become God,
the land of God, heaven, will be built.
A person who has become God
will amass his blessings in the land of God,
which is his and he will live forever with these blessings.
Heaven, earth and man live according to man's will,

and the new heaven and new earth will be created according to
  man's will.
The human mind sees God and man as being separate
but God and man are one,
and completion itself.

A Foreign Place

Many people live scattered around the world,
thousands of miles away from home.

In the past, many tears were shed as people left their homes
for it was thought even a place tens of miles away
was a foreign place.

Even when this tiny country was an agricultural nation,
many people went hungry even though they farmed for a living.
There was a time when we went barefoot
with only tattered clothes on our backs.
Without clothes or shoes
and without enough to eat
people turned their backs on the land of their homes,
and scattered like the wind to cities and countries around the
    world.

China, Japan, Russia, America, Europe,
South America, North America, Asia, Middle East;
there was nowhere they did not go.
For Truth, coincidentally yet inevitably,
Korean people went to all corners of the world.

Past the first generation, and the second,

there are places now with third generation Koreans,

and some with the second generation.

There are some places where the original immigrants still live.

They lived their lives with Korean minds,

but their bones will probably be buried in foreign soil.

We speak the same language,

so they are the springboard

from which Truth will spread.

When they become Truth,

the local people of each country

will study Truth that hails from Korea,

and when they too become Truth,

the world will become a land of one,

and a day will come when all people live a life filled with laughter.

A day will come when the world becomes one,

and all religions unite;

when all people are in heaven while they are living;

when mankind and the Universe become complete

and live forever in a heavenly kingdom.

Birthplace

In my hometown,

larks would trill and the sparrows would chirp.

Although the events of that birthplace

are now all dreams of the past,

they have changed to longing.

Now everyone has left,

and there are not many familiar faces remaining.

The adults of old, have also all passed on.

Steeped in poverty,

the village people had no choice but to farm rice and barley.

There were never enough helping hands on the farm

where my mother toiled, with my younger siblings and I.

Such toil was the mark of our childhoods.

The sight of children playing without a care in the schoolyard

always filled me with endless longing.

I worked at a neighboring village

and it was always night when I returned home.

My mother and one of my sisters have already passed away,

so most people there are now unfamiliar strangers.

Even when my longing for home takes me back,

there is nowhere for me to stay.

The people who used to sing, and quarrel,

and rush about their chores on the farm,

have now all left for the cities, to foreign places,

following the tide of time.

Only those blinded by civilization remain,

guarding the homestead.

My mind is filled with longing for everyone,

for all those sorry events;

for someone like me who has to wander and roam

thousands of miles in foreign lands,

there is much longing in my heart for my home.

Everyone I knew has gone,

they left silently without words,

but the *Wisu* river in my hometown still flows,

and the trees and mountains are still as they always were.

But countless ages later

even they will change

and long after that,

there will be nothing that remains.

Even when the land itself disappears,

the sky will still remain.

Even when the land itself disappears,

I will still be living.

To tell people they must become

the Energy and Light of the Universe that never dies,

I travel the world.

Let's live -

let's all become the Energy and Light of the Universe,

and live in the land of this existence as one.

Where you are living now is your second birthplace,

and where you are living is your home.

This life is just a transit stop,

so shed your burdens of this life

and let's all rest awhile.

Let's just live and just exist.

A person with many burdens and suffering

has them because he has taken in many minds.

If he lives as these minds order him to,

he is needlessly busy without achieving anything.

This is suffering itself and burden.

Burden is to live inside the conceptions and habits

that is one's self, and this is suffering and sadness.

To all those bearing burden:

Seek Truth and become Truth,

and if you live as Truth,

there is no suffering, burden or sadness;

it is freedom and liberation,

it is the rest of rests,

and it is the way to just live.

There Is No One Alive

Birds are singing,

fish are leisurely playing

and nature, the four seasons, are alive.

Only silent time passes by,

and within it, man ages, sickens, and dies.

Without knowing why, or where he is going,

he departs.

While man lives in the world,

he believes that that is all there is,

and he does not know that he will die.

Although the whole world is complete,

he does not know that it is so,

and he dies with the delusions of his attachments.

There is no one who is alive.

Nightfall brings a pitiful state

for a wanderer with nowhere to go.

There is no one to beseech, and nowhere to go.

He may linger awhile,

before setting off once more into the darkness.

He has forgotten where he must go,

he does not know where he is going

and he has lost the way;
wearily continuing on
dragging his exhausted body.
Without having achieved anything,
without having acquired anything,
everything is a dream of the past.
There was a time when he would whistle as he walked,
a time when he still had strength in his legs,
a time of successes and being acknowledged.
But now that those times have passed,
they too have disappeared.

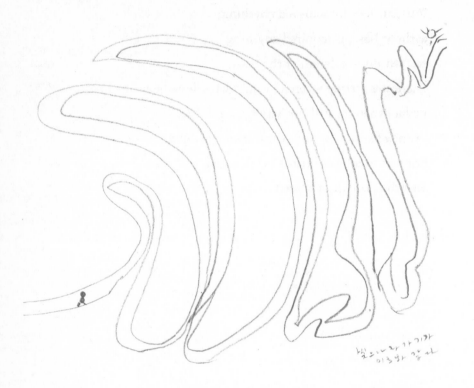

Getting to the Land of Light is like going through a maze.

The Green Mountains Are Mountains

The green mountains are mountains,
and the blue water is water.
A river is a river,
a cow is a cow,
and a pig is a pig.
All things, as they are, are Truth.
People are unable to see things as they are;
they are all insane.
Man is fooled by existence and non-existence,
and he lives inside a mind that is centered around himself.
Man lives without knowing the true meaning
behind dying and disappearing.

A rainstorm is blowing,
and it wets my whole body.
There was joy, anger, sorrow and pleasure
in this futile life.
Now that I have lost everything,
I can reflect back on myself.

What is it to be human,
and what is life,

that people do not know

they live inside a dream

and then pass away into the dream.

When they come to their senses,

it is already too late,

and they depart having given up on themselves.

They pass on to the next world,

without knowing where they go

and only the living finds this pitiful.

When One Becomes Truth

When one becomes Truth,
none of his individual mind exists;
it is when all people return to the original mind of Truth,
that the world will become one.
Then, all will be of one mind,
which is a mind that does not change.
This mind is wisdom itself.
People will live with the mind of one,
and there will be no *you* and *me*.
No longer will there be *your country* and *my country*,
or *your religion* and *my religion*.
Everyone will go to heaven while they are living,
and all will live a life of heaven.
Everything will be done according to nature's flow
and everything will be done with true actions.
People will live according to the perfect solution,
because it exists.
All people will become complete,
and with the mind of one,
they will live for others.

The existence of the sun alone means on Earth

there are some places with one season,

and some with a spring, summer, fall and winter.

If there are cold places, there are hot places also,

and there are places where the temperature is just right, all year round.

Due to their individual minds people blame and fault the events of the world as they live,

but a person who has become the world lives with gratitude.

This exists, and that exists;

everything exists because the world exists

so there is thankfulness for the worth of this existence,

and thankfulness for its ways

when one returns to the origin of the world's profoundness and mystery,

when he returns to the origin of this existence's eminence

for one's self and this existence is one

and all things exist of and by themselves.

Singapore, a man-made *place*,

is only the size of a city

and it is spotlessly clean.

Although it is a good place to live,

it lacks nature.

In the world, there are countries that are well-off,

and also countries that are poor;

in the world there are countless stories,

and there are countless events.

It is within these stories and events that people live

and while it can be said that they live,

no one knows where they are going,

or the reason and purpose of their lives.

There are those that are born, and those that die,

but no one knows the purpose of birth and death.

Futilely and meaninglessly they possess a self,

but they eventually die.

Over in the horizon of the blue sky,

the waves sway silently,

and endlessly they repeat their work.

It is impossible to know when people first started living here in
   Guam

where people ceaselessly come and go.

They all live in their various ways.

Though countless people come and go,

and go and come,

the nature here always stays.

Nature itself may change,

but the sky will always remain, silently.

People live lives that are like the flowing water,

but in the midst of ignorance of life and death's true meaning,

I teach people how to know the ways of the world,

and how to live in the world.

I teach the life of great nature,

and I teach the principles of great nature.

I alone fret that there is no one in the world who knows.

But many people are drawing closer to true knowing

and the loneliness in my heart is slowly lessening.

Until all people in the world become people who know,

I will silently continue to make turfs of knowing.

The ways of the world may be this or that way,

and I live silently, just the way the world is, and the way it can be
    seen,

but people who have much to say, speak ceaselessly

and live lives where nothing remains.

·They blame the years that are futile,

and they take a mind of greed.

A life of nature's flow that follows nature,

can only be had when one becomes nature.

When one is born as the mind of that existence

that is silent and where everything is alive,

everything is one.

Man believes himself to be great,
and lives trapped inside his great self,
so he is blind to the world
and deaf to the words of the world.
He only mutters the sounds of his own self,
and within those meaningless words, he dies.
Without knowing where he will go,
he sighs.

When There Is No Self

When there is no self,
one's mind becomes the Universe;
and he who has become the Universe is without death.
He is the eternal and indestructible Energy and Light.
He who has been reborn as this existence itself
lives in the real world of Energy and Light
forever.

True Freedom

When one sheds his own mind,

and comes to have the true mind,

it is true freedom.

Casting off one's self and becoming Truth

is liberation, which is freedom.

When you do not exist, and you become Truth,

Truth sets you free -

it is the world of Truth, a world of never-changing eternal life,

it is the complete world of Truth.

Everything in the world is eternal and never-changing

because when there is no self,

it is a world of great freedom,

a world where one lives freely for all eternity.

This is the world of Truth, and a complete world.

When man becomes Truth,

and the world exists in man,

when man becomes Truth,

and Truth exists in man,

everyone becomes one,

and this land is heaven and the world of eternal life.

When one is reborn as the Truth that is the Creator,

everyone lives;

everyone is alive.

Truth Inside One's Mind

One speaks according to what his mind holds,

and his actions and life reflect what his mind holds.

A person who has Truth inside his mind

lives as Truth for he has Truth;

and he lives in the land of Truth.

Only one who has Truth can know Truth

and only such a person acts truly.

For him, everything is Truth

and all things live in the completed land of Truth.

Since he has Truth in his mind,

there is no death.

A Dead Life

A dead life is a life of being born and dying;
and such a life is a dream.
Everything is Truth
and everything is alive.

Everything in the world is all nonsense
but there is no one who knows that it is so.
Man's mind is busy
trying to catch clouds and the wind,
but there is nowhere to go or stay -
it is futility itself.
There is nothing man can have,
nothing that remains.
Heaven has appeared
but many remain sleeping, muttering nonsense.
They are woken and woken again,
but their sleep is so deep,
they are unable to awake.

Truth And Falseness

It is said that the moon drifts with the clouds;

and people live this way,

but on a clear day, though the clouds may drift over the sun,

the sun does not move.

Man lives in darkness,

and no one knows the moon does not move.

The way man lives is back - to - front -

there are times when areas of shade become areas of light

and times when light becomes shade.

There are times when the rich become poor,

and there are times when the poor become rich.

There are times in the world,

when those with sufferings, burdens and hardships

become successful and come into good times.

It is a way of the world that there will be times

when the wealthy meet truly difficult times.

No one knows Truth or falseness.

Only a person who has become Truth

knows both falseness and Truth.

All Is Well

All is well,
everything in the world is well.
After a life of suffering and burden,
tears and blame, and babbling about my worth,
I have woken from the dream.
All of it was a futile dream.
Now that I have woken, all is well.
Now that all have woken from a long sleep -
parents, siblings, spouses and children -
all is well.

In the past, I was right and you were wrong,
and I tried to make the world fit myself,
but it could not because the world did not exist inside me.
Now I have become the world,
I see everything in the world is right.
Living in mutual harmony,
all is well.
John and Jane, the old and young, the wealthy and poor,
the great and the foolish - these are all human affairs
but when all people become the world,
everyone is all well.

All is well.

I, who did not know where I came from,

why I lived, or where I would go,

now that I know everything,

all is well.

I did not know life and death,

but I have woken from the dream

and now that I know the principles of life,

I know I, and not the world, was wrong.

I have repented and my conceptions have been born anew,

thus all is well.

I was to blame for everything, everything was my fault.

Things exist as they are, as one sees and hears them,

and the futility of immaturity is gone,

thus, the world is well.

It is good-looking, it is well-born and it truly lives well.

Truth is within me while I am living;

I have heaven and I do not die,

so all is well.

Everyone welcomes the sound of raindrops

falling in a new heaven and earth that is life.

It is the water of life for a thirsty world.

That exists because *this* exists

and through the providence of events, all creations exist.

The creations of the world came into creation

because existence exists.

Everything lives according to the providence of the world,

and death comes when through the providence of the world,

the span of life comes to an end.

Man's mind was made to resemble the Creator,

thus, one who has the mind of the Creator does not die.

The world is already all alive and complete.

It lives forever with me, within me.

One speaks and lives as much as one has,

man speaks and lives according to what he holds in his mind.

He who has delusions within him, lives delusionally,

and he who holds Truth in him, lives as Truth.

He who has this mind has eternal heaven in his mind,

the land that lives forever,

therefore he has been born in heaven and he will live.

His mind is Truth itself so he lives in the land of Truth,

and he is born as Truth from the whole that is Truth.

The land of Truth is his mind,

and he himself lives as Truth.

Truth

For so many ages,

there was no Truth.

Because it did not exist,

people did not know Truth.

Truth cannot be seen by human eyes,

and it cannot be heard;

man did not have Truth

because he did not have it in his heart.

Just as man knows only as much as what exists within him,

only he who has Truth in his mind knows Truth.

The Existing Sky

Though there may be clouds in the sky,
the sky itself just exists.
Regardless of whether countless celestial bodies exist,
the sky itself just exists.
Whether or not people exist,
and whether or not all creations exist,
the sky itself just exists.
A person for whom this sky has become him,
lives in the land of heaven.

Real And False

Heaven and earth exists within man;

within man, in man, heaven exists.

It exists when man completely abandons himself.

In a world that has become the playground of falseness,

there is nothing that is real.

That which is real knows falseness

as well as what is real,

but that which is false believes that

it will go to heaven -

it does not know that heaven is a place

where only real entities live.

No one knows that he is a non-existent illusion

and that he lives in a hell from which he can never awaken

if he, at present, is false and not real.

Countless religions bicker that they are real and true,

but no one knows if he is not real, now,

he is dead and unable to go to heaven

because he is not real.

The land of heaven must be had while one is living,

and it can only be had if one is real,

but a person who is false cannot know this principle.

Truth is a living existence, and one that is complete,

and only a person who has become this very existence lives in
eternal heaven.

He who insists that only what is his is right,

cannot possibly know that he is wrong.

He who goes to eternal heaven

discards his false self and the false world;

he becomes real, and goes to the real land while he is living,

but he who is unable to go does not realize

that for him eternal life and heaven do not exist.

Those who are false believe someone will come

and take them to heaven,

but to "take" someone is to teach them to discard their false selves,

and the teacher is the Savior.

They do not know this person is the one who will take them,

and they believe that the real existence will come

and take their false selves to heaven.

They are deep inside that dream of waiting,

and they live with that dream

because falseness does not have wisdom.

When Jesus came two thousand years ago

the Jewish people who were bound to the Old Testament

did not believe he was the son of God,

and they still do not believe he is the son of God;

in the same way, a person who is in his dream

waits for a delusional God and is unable to know.

Even though a person whose consciousness is Truth exists,

though a person of Truth has come to the world,

man can only see the outward form,

and cannot see the person of Truth.

The person of Truth is a living person,

and only a living person can recognize

and distinguish the living from the dead.

The dead know neither the living nor the dead.

Everything is all alive, and heaven already exists,

but man is dead because of his self-centered sins.

Man is false because of his sins and karma

but there is only one sin that exists -

the sin of not becoming Truth.

The eternal and imperishable land is the land of Truth -

a land where only those who have become Truth and real live.

No one knows this -

I would really like them to know,

so that they may repent,

discard their falseness, and become resurrected as real entities;

so that all people may live in the real land of oneness.

Oh foolish people!

Ask yourselves whether you are real,

and if the answer is that you are not,

repent,

so that you may become real.

One's Body Must Be Born As
The Complete Mind Of Truth

The clouds are sleeping.

The clouds are sleeping, silently.

I am the clouds.

There is nothing that is not me.

The sky in America is unbelievably clear.

The sky in Korea is clouded with pollution,

darkened by the dust clouds that blow over from China

but the sky in America is so blue, it is almost black.

Now that my mind has become the sky,

I see that it is neither blue nor black,

but that in the midst of the completely empty sky

where there is absolutely nothing,

the sole God exists.

This God just exists,

and it is the place before the creation of the wind, clouds, and all
    creations,

yet, all creations are this existence itself.

The material and non-material are simply, one.

People only know the material

and they do not know the non-material real existence is the
    material.

Though the material exists, it is the non-material real existence,

and even when the material disappears -

whether the material exists or not -

the non-material real existence always exists.

People do not know this existence

because they do not have this existence inside their minds.

No one knows the master of all things under heaven is this
existence,

and they do not know this existence is the origin of all creations.

I have become this existence,

and I live doing the work in the land of this existence with wisdom.

Man must make his own blessings.

I have made and acquired many blessings, but people have not.

To be completely enlightened means

one becomes one with the sole God of the empty sky and is reborn.

To become completely one with this existence

one must be marked on the forehead, and connected with it,

and when his self is completely gone,

the sole God of the empty sky is one's very self.

Then one's whole body is connected,

there is light from one's whole body,

and one's self of this existence has become the complete existence
itself.

This is what one must be enlightened of.

Then there is absolutely nothing that he knows and he just lives, and yet he is the absolute Truth.

Such a person is without any inadequacies or deficiencies,

he is the God of wisdom itself,

and he lives doing the work of heaven.

Maum Meditation Centers
Location And Contact Details

Please visit www.maum.org for a full list of addresses, phone and fax numbers,
as well as the locations and contact details of over 240 South Korean regional centers.

[South Korea]
Nonsan Main Center
82-41-731-1114

[U.S.A.]
AK
Anchorage
1-907-865-5954
CA
Berkeley
1-510-526-5121
Diamond Bar
1-909-861-6888
Irvine
1-949-502-5337
L.A. (Downtown)
1-213-484-9888
L.A. (Koreatown)
1-213-908-5151
Long Beach
1-562-900-5585
Orange
1-714-521-0325
San Diego
1-858-886-7363
San Fernando
Valley
1-818-831-9888
San Francisco
1-650-301-3012
San Jose
1-408-615-0435
CO
Denver
1-303-481-8844

FL
Miami
1-954-379-6394
GA
Atlanta
1-678-683-4677
Smyrna
1-678-608-7271
HI
Honolulu
1-808-533-2875
IL
Chicago
1-888-979-6286
MA
Boston
1-617-272-6358
MD
Ellicott City
1-410-730-6604
NC
Raleigh
1-919-771-3808
NJ
Palisades Park
1-201-592-9988
Teaneck
1-201-801-0011
NV
Las Vegas
1-702-254-5484
NY
Bayside
1-718-225-3472
Flushing
1-718-353-6678

Manhattan
1-212-510-7052
Plainview
1-516-644-5231
PA
Elkins Park
1-215-366-1023
TX
Austin
1-512-585-6987
Dallas
1-469-522-1229
Fort Worth
1-817-581-6286
Houston
1-832-541-3523
Plano
1-972-599-1623
VA
Arlington
1-703-354-8071
Centreville
1-703-815-2075
WA
Federal Way
1-253-520-2080
Lynnwood
1-425-336-0754

[Argentina]
Almagro
54-11-4862-5691
Flores
54-11-4633-6598
Floresta
54-11-3533-7544

[Australia]
Perth (Mandurah)
61-8-9586-2070
Perth (Vic Park)
61-8-9355-4114
Sydney
61-2-9804-6340

[Brazil]
Aclimacao
55-11-2537-5725
Brasilia
55-61-3877-7420
Sao Paulo
55-11-3326-0656

[Cambodia]
Phnom Penh
855-78-901-434

[Canada]
Mississauga
1-289-232-3776
Montreal
1-514-507-7659
Toronto
1-416-730-1949
Vancouver
1-604-516-0709

[Chile]
Santiago
56-2-2813-9657

[Colombia]
Batan
57-1-487-4680

Medellin
57-4-230-5001
Palermo
57-1-474-5202

[England]
London
44-208-715-1601

[France]
Paris
33-1-4766-2997

[Germany]
Berlin
49-30-2100-5344

[Guatemala]
Guatemala City
502-2360-6081

[Hong Kong]
852-2572-0107

[Hungary]
Budapest
36-1-950-9974

[India]
Gurgaon
91-97178-63915

[Indonesia]
Tangerang
62-21-5421-1699

[Italy]
Genova
39-349-364-2607
Milan
39-2-3940-0932

[Japan]
Fukuoka
81-92-406-7588
Kyoto
81-75-708-2302
Osaka
81-6-6777-7312
Saitama (Omiya)
81-48-729-5787
Sendai
81-22-762-9462
Tokyo (Machiya)
81-3-6806-6898
Tokyo (Shinjuku)
81-3-3356-1810
Yokohama
81-45-228-9926

[Kazakhstan]
Almaty
7-775-651-98-34

[Kenya]
Nairobi
254-20-520-3346

[Laos]
Vientian
856-20-2817-2400

[Madagascar]
Antananarivo
261-34-9120-308

[Malaysia]
Johor Bahru
60-7-361-4900
Kuala Lumpur
60-12-920-2792

[Mexico]
Mexico City
52-55-5533-3925
Tijuana
52-664-380-8109

[Myanmar]
Yangon
95-94-2113-9996

[New Zealand]
Auckland
64-9-480-7245
Christchurch
64-3-358-7247

[Paraguay]
Asuncion
595-21-234-237

[Philippines]
Clark
63-45-624-7858
Manila
63-2-687-1294

[Russia]
Moscow
7-495-331-0660

[Singapore]
Marine Parade
65-6440-0323
Tanjong Pagar
65-6222-4171

[South Africa]
Pretoria
27-12-991-4986

[Sweden]
Stockholm
46-76-804-6806

[Taiwan]
Taipei
886-989-763-445

[Thailand]
Bangkok
66-2-261-2570

[Vietnam]
Hanoi
84-169-698-1968
Ho Chi Minh City
84-8-5412-4989

[Uganda]
Kampala
256-784-820-724